Racing to Keep Up:

Talking with your kids about technology use and strategies to protect the home computer

Marje Monroe, MSW

Doug Fodeman

First published by Dog Ear Publishing
4010 W. 86th Street, Ste H
Indianapolis, IN 46268
www.dogearpublishing.net

ISBN: 978-159858-986-3

This book is printed on acid-free paper.

Printed in the United States of America

Contents:

Children Online: Realities, Issues and Solutions

Our innovative and unique approach to technology education combines the latest technological information within a framework of understanding child and adolescent behavior. With a clear understanding of the social and emotional impact of technology on children and teens, we explore the ways children and teens are vulnerable and at-risk online and on their cell phones. We provide parents, children and educators with concrete information and realistic, workable strategies to tackle the challenges of negotiating the technological world.

Children Online began in 1997 with a phone call from Doug Fodeman to Marje Monroe asking for help with an issue concerning online bullying. Marje, who was the Upper School Counselor at Buckingham, Browne and Nichols School, had begun researching this issue. Word of our unique and collaborative program quickly spread and we were soon invited to visit other schools. Since 1997 we have researched issues affecting children online and spoken to thousands of students and their parents at schools, churches, synagogues and youth organizations across the United States and abroad. With more than 50 years combined teaching experience, we are also experts working with young people and schools.

Marje Monroe is a Clinical Social Worker and educator with more than 20 years of counseling, programming and teaching experience in schools. Marje's professional experience includes Dean of Students at Stoneleigh Burn-  ham School in Greenfield, Massachusetts; Upper School Counselor at Buckingham Browne and Nichols School in Cambridge, Massachusetts; Upper School Counselor at Garrison Forest School in Maryland; Director of Counseling at St. Andrew's School in Boca Raton, FL; Counselor and Substance Abuse Coordinator at Wittenberg University. Throughout her career, Marje has taught Advanced Placement Psychology, English and developed curricula on sex education, substance abuse, ethics and decision-making. Coordinating schools, families and community agencies on behalf of the well-being of children and adolescents, Marje is proactive and helps schools and families work together to promote the qualities of school and home life that nurture the healthy, social and emotional development of children.

Doug Fodeman is currently the Director of Technology at the Brookwood School in Manchester, Massachusetts. He has taught high school science for more than 18 years, served as Director of Technology at the Pingree School, and served as a technology consultant to the architectural firm  Olson, Lewis, Dioli & Doktor, focusing on the integration of computer technology into architectural design. Doug has also given workshops on a wide variety of related topics such as

"Using Search Engines Effectively," "Protecting Your Privacy Online," and "Telecollaboration." Doug has made appearances on the *ABC Nightly News* and the *CBS Evening News* in regard to cell phone scams targeting children. He has also been a guest speaker with Deborah Rowe of the ABC affiliate WLSAM Radio in Chicago on the topic of cell phone scams targeting children and issues affecting children online. Together with Marje Monroe, they have appeared twice on *The Jordan Rich Show* on WBZ in Boston.

www.childrenonline.org

"Your father and I are going out. This is MZ-7000 and he is going to keep an eye on your internet activity until we get the parental control software updated on the computer."

Illustration by David Saunders. www.DavidThomasSaunders.com

Introduction

There is one unchanging truth about life online, whatever children are doing today they will be doing it at a younger age next year. In 2000, it was unusual for sixth graders to have their own email accounts and unsupervised access to the Internet. Today, parents and children report that second and third graders have email and instant messaging accounts. The average age of children using and experimenting with the Internet gets younger and younger each year. With the popularity of sites such as Webkinz and Club Penguin, children as young as five or six are being introduced to the idea of chatting and social networking online. Young children who are beginning to understand the structure and rules of language are faced with online communication that has its own grammar, language and rules. Children who are just beginning to form friendships outside the home are faced with bullying, harassment and secret-sharing online. Children are facing issues and concepts online that they are not emotionally or chronologically ready to negotiate. Six-year-olds on Webkinz, for example, have had their online "bedrooms" and "playrooms" trashed or "stolen" by pranksters. This can cause a great deal of stress and upset for children who do not understand the risks and just want to play with their stuffed animals.

It is almost impossible for parents to keep up with their kids. Today's kids see the Internet as a seamless part of their culture. For teens, texting and chatting have become their main forms of communication. Scrolling chat rooms and hanging out on social networking sites have replaced walking through the mall.

For affirmation on how technology is transforming our children's lives, simply look at the evolution of the cell phone. Just 10 years ago, the cell phone was a portable telephone. Today, cell phones connect to email, send text messages, cruise the web, pay bills, take and send photos and digital video, are used for spying or cheating in school and fold up to slide into a shirt pocket. In 1922, Thomas Edison said, "I believe that the motion picture is destined to revolutionize our educational system and that in a few years it will supplant largely, if not entirely, the use of textbooks." No doubt his remarkable statement was inspired by access to information in a way that was revolutionary in the classroom. Though Mr. Edison's claim never came true, he nonetheless recognized the tremendous value of information and technology. Our children, however, don't see the Internet and the technology as tools for information and technology. They see it as an integral part of their social life, linking them to friends and attention.

Though we may not always be able to keep up with our children's technological skills, we are and always will be the keeper of our family values and ethics. Most children and teens forget their values when in front of a screen. Very kind, gentle children can turn to bullying, meanness and scapegoating lured by the anonymity behind their screens. As much of the language and tone of emails, instant messages and text messages are increasingly harassing and aggressive; children are becoming desensitized to harassing and mean language.

From the safety of their homes, children are venturing online into a world filled with fun, information, connections, friends and adventure. From their homes, our children are also being exposed to harassment, cruelty, marketing scams, inappropriate material including pornography and risks of exposing personal information to strangers leading to identity theft or worse. As parents, we understand and caution our children about crossing streets, venturing into strange neighborhoods, communicating with strangers in public or driving the car too fast. It is much harder for parents to caution and educate children about the risks of venturing into the world of technology.

This book helps parents and adults better understand the technology our children are using and provide workable strategies for creating rules and structure for our kids.

Chapter 1

"You Won a Free iPod"!
Information and strategies for children under the age of 10

Today's children are technologically savvy at a young age. A 3-year-old may know how to use a mouse and keyboard before she can write her name. Computers and cell phones are as much a part of their lives as chalkboards and recess. In contrast, many adults are using the technology as a tool. Many adults do not rely on the Internet for their communication or for forming friendships. But our kids are doing just that.

With the amazing growth of the Internet, parents are left trying to comprehend how their children's lives will be affected. Fifteen years ago it was unthinkable to imagine children communicating with strangers online with the ability to have a live chat or video chat conversation. Now our children have access to this technology in cleverly marketed sites designed to lure children to explore the Internet. Adults without the reference or knowledge about the technology or the workings of the Internet may find it very frustrating and daunting to guide their children through these sites.

Thousands of websites today are marketing heavily to young children hoping to introduce them to the idea of gaming, chatting, and purchasing items online. Children eagerly tell stories of winning a free laptop and "chasing the moving iPod." And though they all "click to win," giving out personal information when asked, the children also agree that no one actually wins the laptop. Still, they continue chasing the fun, colorful and exciting pop-ups. Asking young children to avoid alluring sites or clever pop-ups can be impossible. It is especially important for parents of young children to be vigilant in helping their children begin to negotiate their online experience as the children may not be ready developmentally to structure their own time online.

Young children with email accounts are being exposed to inappropriate language, lack of grammar rules and acronyms instead of words just when they are learning to read and write and explore language. Grammar rules such as punctuation, spelling and syntax are eroded online. As children spend more and more time communicating online, the important communication skills taught at home and in school are forgotten. As there are free email accounts available everywhere online, many children have accounts that are hidden from adults and schools. We find that by the fifth grade, most children admit to having two different email/instant messaging accounts. Some children can have multiple accounts for gaming sites, social networking sites, email accounts and instant messaging accounts.

Given the freedom online, it is only a matter of time before children are exposed to bullying, harassment, inappropriate language or pornography online. At every school we go to, the younger students all agree that it is easy to be mean online. They also tell us that because they are not face to face while "talking" they don't feel as bad about saying mean or insulting things. A mom whose 10-year-old daughter begged her for an email account gave in with an email account restricted to her friends despite having misgivings. Two weeks later, her daughter received an email stating, "Barney was raped." The mom was forced to begin trying to explain what the word *rape* meant before she was ready to begin having serious conversations about sexuality and relationships with her child. As often happens online, development is accelerated and children are put at risk.

Websites such as Webkinz, Club Penguin, Runescape and Barbie Online are brilliantly marketed to kids. They are colorful, creative, interactive and very alluring. Even though playing the games on the sites can be fun and educational, it is important to note that these sites do have chatting components. And even if the sites allow strict parental controls and encourage children to be safe and smart, these sites are also getting children excited about the idea of communicating and chatting online. The sites in effect become gateways to YouTube, Facebook and other "adult" social networking sites. In addition, children's sites are often tied to merchandising that can be purchased online or in stores. Webkinz, for example, sells their "pets" in stores across the country and online. Children who use Webkinz every day soon long to be doing "real" chatting on the adult sites such as Facebook or MySpace. In 2003, it was unheard of for sixth graders to have Facebook or MySpace accounts. Today, we know fourth graders with accounts on these adult social network sites.

One of the most popular sites of kids' ages 10 to 18 is YouTube. Although the sites state they are not appropriate for anyone under age 13, young children are seen in videos and chatting with others. YouTube allows users to upload and watch videos and make comments about the videos. Recently the site has become a very popular social networking site. Despite the admonition for users to be 13 or older, it just takes a minute to create an account with a fake birth date. A simple lie with a fake birth date stating the user is over 18 grants immediate access to the 18 and over videos. Parents may not realize that the site encourages postings about videos and unsuspecting kids may upload a video and receive mean or harassing postings about their video.

For example, the following was posted under a video made by a 9-year-old about his Webkinz collection:

webkinz are for freaks myepets and shining stars and kookeys and mushabelly rock webkinz are shit and really 400 dolars for a love puppy thats crap there just retardted little toys really who eber has about 10 or more webkinz get a life

webkinzclub123 *(3 days ago) Show Hide*

Reply
if u dont lke um cool but she is a lil girl what are you 2 u fag she like only 7

YouTube is a phenomenon and has allowed the average person to view amazing videos and historical footage never before possible. As teachers, we often use YouTube for hard-to-find footage for our classes. YouTube is an excellent example of the best and worst of the Internet; amazing access to educational videos and information, along with easy access to pornography, bullying and harassment.

Strategies for Young Children Online

For younger children, create a plan for Internet use that includes sharing an email account with a parent. Begin by emailing relatives or close family friends.

We recommend waiting until age 9 before beginning a shared email account. Parents should be in control of the account password.

Consider putting key logging software on the family computer that tracks all activity online when the child is young.

With this software in place the child grows up understanding the monitoring that parents have over their exploration of the Internet. It is always easier to take away boundaries than to put boundaries in place that did not previously exist.

Install filters and software products that provide structures and boundaries for all users. (See Chapter 13 for recommendations.)

Today's software products are very good and offer parents the ability to limit Internet time, filter out inappropriate language and limit sites that the child can explore.

We recommend that children have restricted access to Webkinz, Club Penguin or other child networking sites until age 9.

Allowing access to these sites at a younger age encourages and trains kids to consider the Internet to be fun and the easiest source for finding friends. When the kids complain about limited time online, encourage group sports, family events, and manipulative games such as LEGOs or puzzles.

We recommend that children not have their own email or instant messaging accounts until at least the sixth grade.

Children are not developmentally ready for the bullying, harassing and/or inappropriate material that they will be faced with by having an email or instant messaging account.

Be clear with children about rules for computer use. Create a family plan that includes room for negotiation as the child grows older.

Include values and ethics when talking about the Internet. Encourage children to be the same online as they are in person and to be kind and respectful.

> *A great deal of the language and communication online is harassing, mean and inappropriate. It is especially important for families and schools to encourage children to be kind, respectful and appropriate when online.*

Encourage children to talk to an adult whenever they feel frightened or uncomfortable about something they encounter online.

> *Research shows that children (especially teens) rarely talk to adults when frightened or scared online. The children often worry that their families will "take away the computer" if they report a problem. Talk to your child; explain your worries and your willingness to work with them to keep them safe.*

Teach your child to avoid providing personal information when asked in pop-ups or advertising.

Chapter 2

"Who's on Your Buddy List?"
Information and strategies for the middle school years

As we all know, or experienced ourselves, middle school can be challenging. From navigating lunchrooms, recess and now online chatrooms, this age group is going through numerous physical, emotional and intellectual changes while struggling to be accepted. The middle school years are filled with questions, vulnerabilities and adventures. Insecure tweens have historically turned to bullying and scapegoating to feel stronger.

Today, the playground bully has moved online away from the watchful eyes of adults. Every middle school student we talk to knows the many ways to "trick" other kids online. It is common for groups of kids to go online impersonating another student or simply sending out mean emails. In its most severe form, harassing behavior has driven victims to depression. Children and teens will stay online despite being harassed believing that they can change the minds of their harassers. More often than not, kids deal with the harassment alone.

The Internet provides anonymity. Kids can hide behind their screen and never face the "buddies" they are communicating with. When kids act cruel online, they don't have many of the normal social cues such as facial expressions and body language that happen in face-to-face settings. Without those social cues, it is easier to feel little guilt or responsibility toward others. Teaching responsibility and respect can be challenging for this age group. Add the anonymity of the Internet and it becomes daunting.

Around the age of 11, the number of kids using instant messaging skyrockets. Kids are drawn to instant access to "friends" with the relative safety of forming relationships without face-to-face contact. The numbers of "friends" on kids' instant messaging buddy lists have become a currency. It is not unusual for 10- to 13-year-olds to have up to a hundred screen names on their lists. Names such as "Cooldude123," "surferchick," "alphaboy," "R2me2" and "soxfan07" fill lists making it very difficult for parents to know whom their children are talking to online. Parents should have frequent conversations about buddy lists and ask their children to eliminate names when necessary.

Because anyone can create any image or persona online, shy, awkward and nervous kids turn confident, bold and fearless when behind the screen. Conversations that would be impossible for some kids in person become easy online. Middle-school-age kids create relationships with "friends" based on this confident and fearless person. The worry, of course, is what happens to the shy kid? What happens when they meet their "friends" in person? Ongoing conversations with your child can help to address this challenge and provide moments to celebrate your child.

Some of the most popular sites among middle-schoolers include YouTube, AddictingGames.com, Runescape.com, Facebook, MySpace, and MiniClip. Increasingly, children in this age group are turning to sites such as Facebook and YouTube and interacting with older teens and adults. Kids long to "grow up" and be able to do what "adults" do. As adults and parents, we hope our children enjoy their childhood without risking exposure to meanness, bullying or inappropriate material that litters the Internet.

Strategies for Middle School Children

As stated previously, we do not recommend access to instant messaging or private email accounts until at least the sixth grade.

Go through your child's buddy list. Ask who each screen name represents. Make sure your child knows (in person) everyone on their buddy list.

Call other parents of kids on your child's buddy list.

> *Parents can work together to create common rules for instant messaging. There is a great sense of consistency and power for parents when their children receive the same rules or messages when talking to friends.*

Sit down and explore the websites your child is using. Discuss the dangers or risks associated with the sites.

> *Sites like Habbo Hotel and Stardoll, for example, are marketed and targeted to young kids, but in fact can have very adult material on the sites including sexually graphic language and harassment. Check for parental controls and set them to the most restrictive settings possible.*

Use software products to help create structure for your child's computer use.

> *See Chapter 13 for recommendations.*

Have frequent conversations with your child about his/her computer use. Ask him/her to talk about what they like most about their online life. What do they worry about?

You might be surprised by the responses. Some children will say very little, and others may share all sorts of stories. However, by having the conversations, children get the message that the parent is interested and invested in their online life.

Create family rules for time limits on computer use. Consider linking computer time to household work or community service.

Help your children to understand that computer and Internet use is a privilege and not a right. Children today are growing up expecting constant stimulation, entertainment and attention and in turn consider having access to television, gaming and the Internet an expectation for their lives.

Create other activities for your child and the family to make up for time lost online.

While it may sound "uncool" to children, consider taking the family on a hike, bowling or to an event or museum. Sure, the kids will probably complain, but let them complain and eventually they will begin to appreciate the time spent with the family.

Do not allow middle-school-age children access to social networking sites such as MySpace and Facebook. (See Chapter 5 on social networking sites.)

Set rules and boundaries for your child around posting pictures or videos of themselves or their friends on sites such as YouTube, Flickr or Photobucket.

Chapter 3

"None of Your Business"
Information and strategies for teens online

Teens today are fluent in all aspects of online communication technology including instant messaging, chat rooms and texting. As Marc Prensky outlined in his book *Digital Natives*, children are digital natives and adults are immigrants. It is astonishing how teens today are experts at multitasking. It is not unusual to find a teen with a cell phone in hand texting, while scrolling Facebook and watching TV. Teens can and do manage six different chat conversations at speeds that are awe-inspiring. Adults might have difficulty participating in one chat conversation, much less six, while texting and keeping up with a Red Sox game.

Though we may not be able to catch up to our teen's technological skills, we are, and always will be, the keeper of our family values and ethics. As parents, we know that teens work hard to define themselves, to individuate and, of course, to push boundaries. As a 14-year-old, I remember being told "no" to attending a party but attended anyway. Sneaking out of the house late at night, I was confident, arrogant and reckless. Luckily, vigilant parents who were more concerned with my decision-making than in being punitive caught me. (Although, I was grounded for quite a while!) Many of my friends were caught when trying to push boundaries and take unhealthy risks. Today's teens are often alone in their risk taking and there are many adventures and risks facing teens online.

As we travel the country meeting thousands of teens, we are constantly struck by their respectful behavior in school, their enthusiastic participation in political debates and their focus on community service. This, however, does not always translate to their behavior online. A small, thin screen covers a lot of territory, creating a void between the teens and the places they explore or the "friends" they communicate with online. The screen acts as a buffer to social consequences and face-to-face realities. Teens, who would not consider using sexually provocative language in person, do it easily and often online. Teens who might be timid or awkward in social settings, find themselves feeling confident and comfortable chatting online. Teens who are responsible, careful, and thoughtful to others in school or at home can be mean, reckless and rude online. Teens often engage in these behaviors because they can. They do this because, for the most part, there are no adults supervising their behavior. There are typically no expectations for behavior online and the anonymity of the screen often removes all sense of social responsibility.

We may not be able to keep up with our teens, but we can set structures and rules for their life online. Creating boundaries or rules on any topic such as driving, homework, or curfew can be challenging at best with teens. However, we continue to set boundaries, hoping they will remember our values and rules when away from our guidance and think twice before acting. We can and should do the same thing for their life online. We can have conversations with our teens, outlining our values and explaining why it is so critical for them to be kind and respectful and careful online. We can create rules around posting photos, using chat rooms, gaming and time spent online. Perhaps the biggest struggle in guiding teens online is their feeling of ownership over technology and the Internet. "It's none of your business" can be a common refrain when asking teens what sites they are visiting or asking about who they are talking to. It *is* our business, however, to keep our children safe and to help guide them through the risks of adolescence.

Strategies for Communicating with Teens

Ignore the eye rolling.

In most teens, it is a natural reflex and adults should not take it personally.

Start conversations with "I" statements.

"I am worried about the dangers on social networking sites" is easier to hear for a teen than "social networking sites are dangerous."

Explain your job as a parent.

When setting rules or structures for teens, tell them why. "It is my job to keep you safe and this is the best way to do that. You might not agree, but I have to do what is best for you and our family."

Stay calm.

Teens can be highly volatile and can change emotions quickly. It is important for parents to stay calm and not get caught up in the moment.

Be consistent.

In some ways, you can compare teens to 4-year-olds. They need constant reminders and reinforcements and will take advantage of any breach in our structure. Let down your guard once and it will take 10 more times of being firm to make up for that one slip.

Look beyond their words.

Often, teens use dramatic language to express their anger. For example, putting time constraints on their online life might elicit the statement, "I hate this stupid rule." However, if you look beyond their words, you might discover that they are scared of being left out of their peer group and feeling insecure.

Validate their knowledge.

Teens love to feel that they know everything. Ask them questions about the Internet. Learn from them and let them feel knowledgeable about the technology.

Remember that you are the expert on parenting.

Though your teen may think they know it all and may, in fact, know a lot more than you about the Internet, you are the expert on raising your child and keeping them safe.

Strategies for Guiding Teens Online

Restrict access to social networking sites such as MySpace and Facebook until age 16.

> *Social networking sites create a wealth of entertainment and socializing online. However, they also contain a wealth of marketing scams, harassing language, invasion of privacy and easy access to pornography with opportunities for poor decision-making and behavior.*

Use software to help create time limits and boundaries for teens.

Challenge your teens to be the same online as they are in person.

> *Today's teens are performing community service, voting in larger numbers than before, and working to create a difference in the world or their own community. Encourage them to begin doing the same thing online and not just resorting to the same bullying, meanness and provocative communication that is typically found throughout the Internet.*

Admit your mistakes and move on.

> *Parents make mistakes. It is the hardest job we will ever have and one without any training manual. If you allowed your teen to have a Facebook account at age*

14 and they are harassed or scammed, tell them you did not realize the risks they face online and now want to help keep them safe.

Be willing to negotiate on rules and boundaries for online use.

The number one reason why teens do not talk to parents about Internet use is their fear that parents will "pull the plug" if they do. Assure your teen that you want to work with them and be fair.

Know your limits.

It is important to know your bottom line for your teen's Internet use. If you do not want them on Facebook until 16, then remain firm on that. Be willing to negotiate in other areas online.

Illustration by David Saunders www.DavidThomasSaunders.com

Chapter 4

Wanna Chat? Life with Instant Messaging

Information and strategies for chat, instant messaging and *online communication*

Millions of children use chat rooms, email and instant messaging to say things that they would not and could not say in person. The anonymity of the Internet makes it easier for children and adults to overstep social norms and etiquette. In today's online world, there are dozens of issues that require parents' attention and intervention on behalf of their children. Many of the risks online affect the emotional and psychological well being of children. It is critical for parents and other adults to help children understand the difference between bullying and teasing or the difference between flirting and sexual harassment. Teens are very vulnerable to meanness as they often read harassing emails as "normal" and "the way everyone talks." Email and instant messaging embolden teens and adults to use strong language and can leave emails vulnerable to misinterpretation.

It is often shocking for adults to read the language in a typical chat room for teens or preteens. Profanity is regularly used and acronyms that may be unfamiliar to adult readers are instantly recognizable to teens. Here are a few examples of commonly used online acronyms:

AYSOS	are you stupid or something?
AYTMTB	and you are telling me this because?
BEG	big evil grin
CRBT	crying real big tears
DKDC	don't know don't care

DHYB	don't hold your breath
DIKU	do I know you?
DIY	do it yourself
GAL	get a life
IMHO	in my humble opinion
IMing	chatting with someone online
IMNSHO	in my not so humble opinion
IPN	I'm posting naked
LMIRL	let's meet in real life
LSV	language, sex, violence
NAZ	name, address, zip
NP	nosy parents
P911	my parents are coming!
PA	parent alert
PAL	parents are listening
PANB	parents are nearby
PANS	pretty awesome new stuff
RUMORF	are you male or female?
RUUP4IT	are you up for it?
SUYF	shut up you fool
TAW	teachers are watching
VEG	very evil grin
WDALYIC	who died and left you in charge?
WTC	want to cyber? (Want to have online sex?)
WTGP	want to go private?

Wherever kids have access to blogging, chatting or texting, you will likely find meanness, harassment and inappropriate language. Consider this snippet of conversation on a popular gaming site:

Marje Monroe / Doug Fodeman

Xman: lkg yr play	(I like your play)
Cchicky: lk yrs	(I like yours)
Xman: IPN	(I'm posting naked)
Cchicky: no sh&t	(Really?)
Xman: you?	(Are you?)
Cchicky: wyltk	(Wouldn't you like to know?)

Language is a reflection of who we are. Can you imagine this conversation happening 10 years ago? Can you imagine this conversation happening face to face? Today, teens see this language as "normal" and so ignore or even encourage provocative comments, threats or sexual innuendo. Looking at the above exchange, it is impossible to know whether or not the players are kids (despite this being a kids' game site) or whether there is a mean, threatening intent. That is the crux of the risk for children. They stay in conversations ignoring threatening remarks and hoping that the other person is, in fact, just teasing and really likes them.

As instant messaging happens live with a speed that boggles adults, children and teens are forced to make snap decisions on language and relationships. Quick replies from an angry fifth grader can, and often, causes distress and anxiety among his or her peers at school. Messages that are provocative or mean get processed so quickly that users put themselves at risk before recognizing the harmful intent. Today, teens are using instant messaging or email to end relationships, resolve conflicts, flirt, or search for intimacy. It is especially important that children and teens realize the danger in resolving conflict online where tone cannot be detected and it is easy to misin-terpret someone's words. By resolving tough relationship issues online, children and teens miss the face-to-face contact that comes with having those conversations in person.

The speed, anonymity and immediacy of the Internet accelerate relationships. Young teens, and even children, reveal intimate details about their life through email, blogs, instant messages or chat rooms. It is not unusual for kids to email each other dozens of times a day or send texts back and forth all day. These conversations may take place without ever meeting each other in person. What then happens for these young people who have established a very emotional connection when they meet in person? What happens when the intense relationships falter and the kids are left feeling hurt and angry? It is often hard for adults to fully recognize the importance of online relationships. They are very real for our kids and can cause very real joy and very real anguish.

Strategies for Instant Messaging and Communication Online

Do not allow instant messaging accounts until at least the sixth grade.

> *Young children are not developmentally ready for the instant decisions they make in live chat. They are easily manipulated and can become targets for bullies or marketing scams.*

Talk with your children about the responsibilities of online communication.

> *Though our children are reminded at home and at school to be kind, respectful and polite in person, often children do not apply this to their relationships online. Challenge children and teens to be the same online as they are*

in person and to stay away from bullying, gossip and meanness.

Keep Internet access in a public location

All experts in online safety recommend keeping Internet access in a public location where parents are able to monitor their children's activity.

Make sure your children actually know their online "buddies."

It is common for kids to have dozens of IM buddies. These buddies may not be anyone they know in person. Go through your child's buddy list and make sure they do not have anyone on their list that they do not know in person.

Contact the parents of the kids on your child's list.

Groups of parents can create common rules for IM usage and try to avoid bullying or meanness. Call parents of IM buddies as you might with play date buddies.

Limit Internet access and time.

Avoid Internet access during dinner hours, study hours or after bedtime. Today's software products can be very useful in helping parents create structures for Internet access.

See Chapter 13 for advice on reliable prod-ucts for both PCs and Macs.

Have frequent conversations with your child about their Internet use.

The best software products cannot replace guidance, concern and advice from parents. Keep engaged with your child's Internet usage. Ask them to show you conversations they have online and remind them to be responsible and thoughtful.

Educate your children on the importance of face-to-face communication.

In order to promote healthy relationships and pursue lifelong connections, it is important for teens to learn to have difficult conversations in person. Do not, for example, allow your young teen to pursue a social or romantic relationship online if they have not had a face-to-face conversation with their "buddy."

Make the rule "no group instant messaging" in your home.

Children or teens gathered around the same computer screen often leads to bullying, gos-sip, tricks or meanness. Do not allow this in your home unless you are nearby and moni-toring their behavior online.

Help your child understand that online communication, such as instant messaging, is a poor choice when tensions are high, friends are emotional or an issue needs to be resolved.

> *Encourage your kids to pick up the phone or talk to their friend in person to respond to emotional issues or conflicts between friends.*

Chapter 5

Social Networks, a World of Opposites

Understanding and negotiating social networking sites where friends are strangers and privacy is public

Social networking sites (SNSs) have quickly become the communication tool of choice for teens. With the popularity of MySpace and Facebook, teens and adults have flocked to these sites looking for connection to others. What started as a unique and creative way to connect to lost friends or create new friends has morphed into a complex, money-driven experience. The social networking sites of today are filled with marketing pitches, marketing scams, phishing attempts and pornography. There are hundreds of networking sites and, recently, popular sites such as YouTube have turned to social networking to lure additional users. Sites such as BlogTV.com allow children to put themselves on live, real-time, Internet TV communicating with strangers.

Though SNSs have a wide variety of technical features, they basically consist of profiles that display a list of friends or buddies who are also users of the system. After joining a SNS, an individual is able to create a profile. A profile is generated that typically includes descriptors such as age, location, interests and an "About Me" section. Most sites also encourage users to upload a profile photo. Some sites allow users to enhance their profiles by adding photos or videos.

Examples of social networking sites:
MySpace, Facebook, Bebo, Blip, Capazoo, Couchsurfing, Faceparty, Flickr, Friendster, Haboo, LinkedIn, LiveJournal,

Webkinz, Neopets, Orcut, Reunion.com, Tagged, Zanga, YahooMash, Hi5, DeviantArt

As children and teens rush to these sites and begin connecting to others, the sites have also become tools for angry, revengeful and distressed teens. Harassing language and bullying are common and children and teens are increasingly putting inappropriate material on their sites. Fake sites attacking teachers, parents, ex-friends or employers have popped up, creating a great deal of anguish for the attacked party. As anyone can create a site and pretend to be another person, it is impossible to block slanderous and mean material from going online. After it's online, it can be extremely difficult to have material completely removed.

One of our biggest concerns with social networking sites is that though they do offer "privacy settings," there is never a guarantee of privacy on SNS or anywhere online. When talking with teens, they proudly discuss their ability to set their sites to private and universally state they are very careful not to let "anyone" into their site. What teens don't realize is that the fine print of these sites explicitly states that the site has the right to archive, copy, retain, transfer or use the material in any way they deem necessary. In essence, any words, images or videos put up on most social networking sites—including My Space, Facebook, and YouTube—by rights, belong to the sites and not to the individual who posted them online. Adolescents making mistakes and pushing boundaries online can, and do, create serious implications for their futures including college admissions, secondary school admissions, employment checks or simply personal humiliation.

Unbeknownst to most teens, they are being targeted daily with marketing scams, phishing attempts and fake sites set up to lure them to malicious or inappropriate sites. Scammers use sophisticated software to gather personal information that can be used for identity theft or impersonation. As the Internet has grown, people have quickly realized the money-making opportunities on social networking sites. Teens and children follow links and pop-ups hoping to win free merchandise, make more friends or gain entry to a cool new world. The lure of an open door is hard to resist and they exist everywhere online. Online, the open doors can lead to fun, wonder and stimulation. They can also lead to spyware, adware, rip-offs, identity theft and manipulation.

Social networking users are ripe targets for adults with harmful or even criminal intent. Pretending to be a cool 16-year-old, any adult or teen can fake a site, ask for entry to thousands of unsuspecting teen pages and gain entrance into their sites. Once on a page of someone belonging to a network, every user in the network is now open for the person to see and/or exploit. Most teens are, in fact, connected to multiple networks such as sports teams, schools or clubs. And even though teens insist they are very careful about admitting strangers onto their SNS page, it is common for children and teens to allow anyone onto their site if that person seems to "like them."

The Ad Council produces several valuable public service announcements relating to the posting of information online in places like social networks. They are worth looking at and sharing with your teens.
Think Before You Post
(http://tcs.cybertipline.com/psa/BulletinBoard_60.mov)
Everyone Knows Your Name
(http://tcs.cybertipline.com/psa/Everyone_60.mov)

Strategies for Social Networking Sites

We recommend that teens 15 and younger not have access to SNSs.

> *Given the numerous marketing scams, exploitation possibilities, access to sexually graphic and harassing language and opportunities for meanness and bullying, younger teens are not ready developmentally to navigate the site safely. Teens are more vulnerable to exploitation and marketing.*

If your teen already has a site, ask them to let you see their pages.

> *Start by giving them a 24-hour notice and then explain that you will ask to see their page from time to time. If the child refuses because of privacy, explain your role as a parent to keep them safe. Tell them that they may only have access to the site if you are allowed to see the site from time to time.*

Read the fine print.

> *Ask your teen to print out the acceptable use policies for the site and then read the fine print. Read it with them to fully understand their privacy and user rights or lack thereof.*

Use software to help you create time boundaries for SNS use. (See Chapter 13 for recommendations.)

> *Given their choice, teens might be online all night. Appropriate software can help parents create limits for Internet use. For example, you can set Internet access to shut off at 10 pm or during dinner time or study hours.*

Explore the various SNSs yourself.

> *Ask your child to help you explore the social network sites if you do not have your own account. Otherwise set up your own account and begin exploring the sites. We recommend you not use your work or home emails to set up accounts online. Use an Internet service such as Yahoo, Hotmail or Gmail to set up temporary email accounts.*

Ignore your child's outrage about privacy, honesty and distrust.

> *It is common for teens to be outraged when they realize that "adults" have been looking at their sites. In reality, the sites are not "private" even when set to a restricted setting. Teens feel a false sense of ownership of the Internet. Be clear about your role in keeping them safe.*

Explain that there is no privacy online, especially on SNSs.

> *Begin by showing your child the actual terms of condition for a popular site such as Facebook or YouTube. Explain that everything online can be copied, archived, or transferred to another site or person. Explain that colleges, future employers and others are, in fact, searching through Facebook and other social networking sites.*

Google word combinations such as "Facebook" and "scams" or "hack" or "attacks" and ask your child to follow links to see how easy it is to hack into accounts or trick users on SNSs.

Remind them that they lose all control of content after it is posted online.

One final note: The Internet is constantly changing, as are the ways that kids are using it. Recently, some middle and high school students have begun to discover online live broadcast TV, known as "social broadcasting." BlogTV.com and Justin.tv are two such sites where a visitor is able to use a built-in video camera to broadcast him or herself live on the Internet. Anyone else can stop by, enter a chat window, and anonymously interact with the person broadcasting. Without any controls, standards or boundaries, this technology can have negative consequences for some children and teens.

Chapter 6

The World of Gaming

Information and strategies for game playing online

An increasing number of children, teens and adults are playing online games. Early application games such as *Pong* and *Spacewar* set the stage for today's interactive and multi-user games such as *World of Warcraft*, *Everquest*, *Halo*, and *Call of Duty*. MMORPGs (Massive Multi-Player Online Role-Playing Games) allow children and teens to spend hours in interactive fun, alone in bedrooms, and at the same time, connecting with others all over the world. For the most part, the world has seen the evolution of gaming simply as new games or toys, and any concern has revolved around rating requirements for violence and appropriateness.

Even today, many adults and parents see these games as toys. In fact, these games present many more challenges than the early video games. The interactive nature of the games offers the chance to "chat" with other users and gives kids the ability to become invested in a community of players. They are stimulating, exciting and engage children and adults intellectually, emotionally, socially and competitively. Many children and teens, and a growing number of adults, are becoming emotionally attached to the games and to the feelings of excitement and competition the game provides. Estimates today place the number of game registrations at around 30 million people. Fifteen million of them are on subscription-paid accounts that require monthly fees for use (Edward Castronova, "Exodus to the Virtual World").

Today's young adults grew up mastering and manipulating technology, not simply using or understanding the technology.

In many ways, they are changing the way kids view fun. Renting a video, for example, might be entertaining, but renting or buying a game can be life transforming. Relationships are made, communities are created and a feeling of connection and pride are cemented simply by playing the game in a community of online gamers. Games today are adventurous, stimulating, mentally challenging, time absorbing and socially fun. And though this can be great for kids, parents need to be aware of the addictive qualities of gaming and the risks of bullying and harassment found in blogs connected to the game.

Simple online games such as checkers, Tic-Tac-Toe or Scrabble have large community forums where the users chat back and forth and comment on the play. This can be fun and stimulating or harassing, mean and threatening. It is very hard for parents to fully trust or understand the "games" their children are playing. One frantic mother called because she previewed a game for her 13-year-old son called *Grand Theft Auto* and found it horrific. The user got points for picking up prostitutes or hitting pedestrians from their "auto." The mother told her son he could not have it. Her concern was that her son saw nothing wrong with the game and wondered why she was so upset. For kids growing up watching violence and sex on screens, games and online, they are becoming desensitized to cruelty, violence or sexually graphic material.

The games of today are not just games. They come with a number of serious challenges. How do parents manage the hours their children spend online? When is too much? What games are "safe" and what are not? As our kids will always push boundaries, it is up to parents to set structures and understand the consequences of "game" playing online.

Strategies for Structuring Online Gaming for Children

Pay close attention to the ratings of games bought from stores.

Games with an M for Mature rating would be inappropriate for children under the age of 17. If you are unsure, preview the game before allowing your child to play.

Visit: http://www.esrb.org/ratings/ratings_guide.jsp

Set limits on the amount of time children can spend gaming online.

This is where software products can help you with games played on the computer. Gaming can be very stimulating and addictive; when left to kids, they often play hours at a time, ignoring schoolwork or family responsibilities. Game systems such as Xbox or PS2 do not come with any parental controls.

Sit down with your children to discuss and negotiate rules for the home around gaming and games with chat components.

Children and teens need to feel a sense of control and it may help to have a discussion about family rules. Though you may want to set more limits than they would like, it can help to compromise on a few issues to help keep your children engaged in the rules.

Consider restricting the chat components available on most games.

Many parents do not know that games come with chatting components, or for a small monthly fee, can be connected to users all over the world. Be very clear with your child about what you will allow and pay attention to the small print on the packaging or website of the game being played.

Consider the age at which your family allows gaming, chatting and MMORPGs.

We recommend that children under the age of nine do not use computer games with any chatting component. That includes Webkinz or other child-oriented sites. For the more mature MMORPGs we recommend that children not be allowed to play until at least age 12. Parents should then pay special attention to violence and sexually explicit material when choosing games for their child.

Educate your child on the potential risks and dangers associated with MMORPGs and online gaming.

A few important topics to cover are: the interaction with strangers on the chatting sites, getting lost in a "persona" when playing a game, the violence and graphic material found on games; revealing personal information.

Chapter Resource:

Castrovona, Edward. Exodus to the Virtual World: How online fun is changing reality. Palgrave Macmillan. 2007.

Chapter 7

"You Texted Her How Many Times?"

Information and strategies for cell phones and texting

Today's teens use their cell phones as handheld computers giving them access to email, instant messaging, videos, music, games and, of course, texting. Texting has quickly become the mode of communication for young people. It is common for teens to text each other all day, interrupting school, family events and sleep. Unsuspecting parents often realize the extent of texting only after receiving a very large phone bill or with an extensive amount of texts being sent per month.

Text messaging, or texting, is the common term for sending text messages from mobile phones. It is available on most digital mobile phones. Today, the vast majority of texting is used as a social tool by teens and young adults. Young teens are seamlessly using texting as a form of making and sustaining friends and can text at speeds that are mind-boggling to adults.

Many teens tell us that they would rather "text" a break-up than have a phone or face-to-face conversation. Texting, even shorter and quicker than instant messaging, is addictive to young people craving attention and connections. It is a powerful feeling to receive numerous texts and know that someone is thinking about you. It is immediately reinforcing and encourages continued use, creating pathways to addiction. For many children and teens, texting has replaced quick phone calls. For example the text, "ETA: 10pm" eliminates the need to call your friend to say you will arrive at 10 pm.

Few adults realize that there are a wide variety of marketing scams targeting young people who use text messaging. Ads for texting services are often found on children's television channels such as Nickelodeon. Ringtones are sold through text messages, as are jokes-of-the-day. Innocently, kids select a joke; not knowing that through the small print they just signed up for a $9.99-a-week program. It is quite difficult to fight the outrageous costs of programs and gimmicks that kids are drawn to on their phones. It can take months for a phone company to agree to take a charge off the phone. In addition, unscrupulous companies trick teens and tweens into signing up for services even when they push "cancel" or select "no." This practice is called cramming. The charges are masked on cell phone bills where they may appear as generic terms such as "data," "download" and "premium services."

Teens may not realize the hazards of texting. Children and teens have little concept of time when they are online or are texting and can lose large amounts of time chatting by cell phone or instant messaging. Older teens are now risking accidents by texting while driving. It is very distracting to be reading messages and replying while driving a car and listening to loud music. Kids have commonly used texting to cheat on tests and carry on conversations during family gatherings or lectures in school.

Strategies for Text Messaging

Consider buying a phone without Internet or texting capabilities for your children.

> *For the most part, parents give their children cell phones for safety reasons. Children, however, want the phones for fun and connection to friends. With*

computers at home and schools, children and teens do not need Internet access on their mobile phones.

Go online or into stores to investigate the possibilities of phones without texting or with limited texting access.

It is difficult to remove extra phone services after they are purchased. If possible, do research before buying a cell phone package.

Set limits for your child/teen and follow up.

Allow a limited amount of texting and follow-up with the phone bill. For example, you can purchase a package that allows 100 text messages a month for a fee. Though your child can go over that number, the phone bill will show that and charge more money.

Have clear consequences for teens who push boundaries.

Take away access to the phone, for example, if they abuse their texting privileges. Follow through every time and create meaningful consequences.

Encourage responsible and thoughtful communication through text messaging.

As with instant messaging and networking sites, it is easy to send mean or provocative messages. Educate your children about the importance of being responsible and respectful while texting.

Do not allow text messaging until the age of 14.

> *Young children are not ready developmentally for the instant decisions they make while texting. They are easily manipulated and can become targets for bullies or marketing scams. Children are vulnerable and easily hurt by mean comments through text. Texting has quickly become a vehicle for bullying or teasing.*

Do not allow your children to drive and use their cell phone.

> *Teen drivers are most at risk for accidents. Use of cell phones or texting while driving can have deadly consequences.*

Chapter 8

"Don't Worry Mom, I'm Careful"
Information and strategies for negotiating online privacy

The concept of privacy has changed remarkably in the last few years. Reality shows, access to video cameras in cell phones and the website YouTube, have changed our expectations of privacy and intimacy. The truth is that very little is private anymore and nothing online is private. That is a difficult concept for children and teens to comprehend. As adults, we grew up with an expectation of privacy. We made mistakes and didn't worry that they would be broadcast for others to see.

Teens today play out their mistakes online, in blogs, on Facebook and in videos on YouTube. Online pictures of high school and college students drinking have led to discipline in schools and denied admissions to colleges. Children, especially young teens, are very impulsive and the nature of the Internet plays right into this vulnerability. Hiding behind a screen, teens make split-second decisions that seem innocent and relatively risk-free. However, as we noted earlier, the anonymity of the screen makes it easier for kids to put themselves at risk when communicating or responding to online ads or contact from those who try to manipulate and take advantage of them.

Clever marketing and questionable business practices flourish online. Children easily offer private information when thinking they are getting something for "free." Sites offering free products may in fact be downloading viruses or spyware onto your child's PC. (Note: Macs are currently not susceptible to 99% of spyware or adware). Children often provide information such as email address, home address, cell phone number, or even their mother's maiden name, not realizing the dangers of providing this information. Unscrupulous individuals may scour social networking sites looking for private information to use against kids or to get into their parents' bank accounts. Many parents use personal information such as a child's name or birth date as their password to various financial accounts. Hackers use software specifically created to hack into accounts with this information.

With children today bombarded by reality shows such as *Big Brother*, *Survivor*, *Jerry Springer* or *Real Life*, there is a feeling of "anything goes." The good, bad, humiliating, horrific and tragic aspects of life are played out daily for kids to absorb. It is critical for parents to help their children understand boundaries and etiquette. There are very few, if any, role models online that are thoughtful, respectful and careful. Making fun of someone on instant messaging may seem innocent and fun, but in reality, people can and do get hurt. Relationships can be strained or lost due to the mistaken idea of online privacy.

Ask a group of fourth graders if they know anyone who has shared their password and up goes every hand in the room. Kids and teens commonly share passwords with "best friends." This can, and often does, lead to kids using another's account to send out false messages or to read private email. Even a private email sent from one friend to another can be forwarded or printed out for anyone to see. A questionable picture put on Facebook may, in fact, never be completely deleted and may have been archived or copied by someone else. In other words, when posting anything online or in a text message, children and teens must assume that someone else might see their words. Most of them do not assume this, or if they do, they shrug it off, saying, "I'm fine. Nothing will happen to me."

Strategies for Helping Negotiate Online Privacy for Your Children

Tell your children that nothing online is private. Explain the many different ways their privacy may be invaded.

> *Show the reality of privacy on social networking sites by reading to them the small print. Tell them the dangers of information put online today that they wouldn't want seen in five years.*

Teach your child about the importance of creating strong passwords.

(See Chapter 10 for recommendations and more information.)

Tell your children to only buy items online when you are with them.

> *Make sure you are on a secure site where the browser reads "https:." You should also see a picture of a lock in the right-hand corner of your web browser. Sites that have a history and a physical storefront tend to be safer. Amazon.com, Gap.com, etc.*

Explain the concept of archiving.

> *Help your child understand that everything posted or written online may be seen or used by someone else. Companies today exist to copy and archive everything written online for future use and sale of information.*

Explain that though they may trust their best friend today, it is best to keep their passwords to themselves.

> *Passwords are the single biggest reason why children and young teens become targets for identify theft or bullying. When kids share passwords to their accounts, they open up and expose themselves to tricks, bullying or worse. Help your child understand the importance of privacy.*

Encourage the use of an alternative email account for signing up for accounts for purchasing, playing games or using social networking sites.

> *Encourage your child to create a separate account for purchasing or gaming and keeping their personal account separate.*

Encourage family members to protect the privacy of personal email addresses.

> *Tell your children not to use the auto-fill (auto-forms) feature of any web browser. If a business or online form asks you for an email address, for example, tell your family to use the disposable address you created at Yahoo.com or Gmail.com.*

Never publish your private email address on web sites or in online discussion groups.

Chapter 9

Teaching Our Children to Be "Advertising Savvy"

Understanding how our children are targeted and teaching them to avoid the traps

Over the years, we have surveyed thousands of children, ages 8 to 18, about their use of the Internet and communications technologies such as cell phones. If we were asked to sum up all of their collective interests into the most common points it would be:

- To connect to others

- To play games

Scammers and marketers know this as well, and that is why they heavily target kids in their social networks and gaming sites. In this chapter, we will focus on advertising that targets kids on the hundreds of "free" and popular game sites such as FreeGames, AddictingGames, CrazyMonkeyGames, DragonGamez, FreeArcade, and HotGames.com. Many game sites have recognizable, and legitimate, ads linked to well-known vendors, whereas others are highly deceptive, manipulative or outright dangerous because they lead the visitor to drive-by downloads of spyware or adware. Some ads and/or downloadable applications and browser plug-ins lead to hijack-ware that steals control over a visitor's web browser. Though this has been a known threat against PCs for many years, Macs have recently been successfully targeted by hijack-ware as well.

We have visited dozens of popular web sites designed to attract adults and we rarely see the kind of scamming and manipulative ads that populate kids' gaming sites. Many of these game sites primarily attract children between the ages of 10 and 13. Yet many of the ads that compete for their attention contain very small print stating that participants of the offer "must be over the age of 18."

Why is it that so many manipulative and fraudulent ads target children's gaming sites? A glimpse into child and adolescent behavior of children makes this easy to understand:

- Children are often gullible

- Children are impulsive in their behavior

- Children are not savvy about marketing and may be easily manipulated

- Children want to believe that they have won something

- Children do not understand the potential threats that exist online

- Children don't understand the dangers that come from loss of privacy

Here is an example of an ad from a gaming site that is clearly meant to be game-like itself and attractive to kids:

If viewers click the "Push" button fast enough, they will beat the opponent and then are immediately told that they have won a gift:

After we selected the pink iPhone, we were taken to another pop-up ad that asked for our email address. These types of "free" offers begin by asking the visitor for small bits of personal information. Clicking "Submit," "Next" or "Continue" leads to more offers and screens asking for more personal information. What also makes this ad suspicious is that Apple Computer, the manufacturer of iPhones, had not produced a pink iPhone at the time this ad was displayed.

One thing is certain, if you enter the information they request with the hope of receiving your free gift, you will have given away a tremendous amount of private/personal information that is likely used to spam you or worse.

If the visitor enters an email address and clicks "Continue," the following two ads appear:

We had to pass through a gauntlet of seven surveys and were finally told that to claim our prize we had to complete three additional marketing surveys. After suffering more than 12 screens requesting our personal information, we were no closer to receiving our gift. Adding insult to injury, upon closing the browser window we received three more pop-ups telling us we had won 12 additional items.

These ads say they come from WebRewardStream.com. Sites like WebRewardStream target children, especially younger children, because children will often give away a great deal of

information in exchange for a reward or gift. Children typically do not understand the value of personal information in the context of privacy. Also, most children don't know about or understand the ramifications of identity theft. We have actually seen similar ads on other sites asking the visitor for their mother's maiden name!

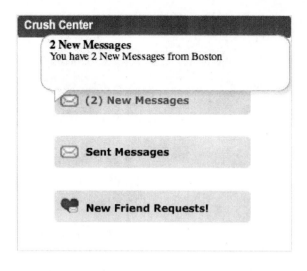

Here is another typical ad found on a gaming site; this one taken from DragonGamez. It appeals to our earlier point that kids increasingly use the Internet to connect to others. Some children, and even teens, may be tricked into thinking that someone who knows them is trying to contact them. It is also made to resemble a "friend message" from Facebook, a very popular social network with teens.

Clicking the ad from the previous page leads to the following image…

Just because a website is designed to appeal to children, doesn't mean that the ads are age appropriate. This soft-porn image was a link leading to additional pornography provided by Zango.com. Both McAfee and Symantec describe Zango as an adware downloader, and several bloggers have said that Zango is linked to teen pornography. Zango.com is an ad provider on many children's web sites. Ben Edelman, who is a leading anti-spyware researcher, has written a report on Zango.com. Read what Ben has to say about the media Zango provides. [http://www.benedelman.org/news/052808-1.html] If you suspect that your computer has been "hit" by Zango's adware, learn how to remove it from the support staff at PCHell.com [http://www.pchell.com/support/zango.shtml] The FTC called Zango one of the largest distributors of adware in 2006. [http://www.ftc.gov/opa/2006/11/zango.shtm]

Arriving at FreeArcade.com, we were told that we were the one-millionth visitor and a winner of a free Dell XP laptop.

After clicking another game-like ad at FreeArcade, we were told that we had won 25 "free" ringtones. The fine print on this ad from Flycell.com actually says that our cell phone would be charged a $9.99/month subscription fee in order to get the ringtones.

There are lawsuits by Attorneys General from many states against companies like Flycell.com. Visit the Ripoff Report and check out what consumers are saying about the fraudulent practices of this company. [Visit www.RipOffReport.com and enter "Flycell" into the search field.]

This list of fraudulent, deceitful scamming ads on children's web sites is endless. Many lead to spyware, adware and inappropriate content. Just because a website is designed for children doesn't mean that it is a safe place for them to explore. Our recommendation is that parents have a conversation with their children about the gaming sites they use. Visit the sites with your children and talk about the advertising that is marketed at them. Teach them:

never to give out personal information
- if it seems too good to be true, it is

- just because you CAN click on it, doesn't mean you should

- not everyone on a child's game site has their best interest in mind

CAN YOU PREDICT WHO SPAMS AND WHO DOESN'T,

WHO TARGETS THE VISITOR WITH MALWARE AND WHO DOESN'T?

Think you can predict how well your privacy is respected on a web site? Which web site will sell your information to spammers? Take MacAfee's Site Advisor spam quiz [http://www. siteadvisor.com/quizzes/spam_0806/]

Can you tell which websites will attempt to install spyware or adware without your knowledge or permission? Take MacAfee's Site Advisor Spyware Quiz. [http://www.siteadvisor. com/quizzes/spyware_0306.html]

Chapter Resources:

OnGuardOnline.gov provides tips from the U.S. government and technology industry to consumers to help them guard against Internet fraud and protect themselves and their personal computer.

OnGuard's quick facts and information about spyware:

http://www.onguardonline.gov/topics/spyware.aspx

Play one of OnGuard's games to raise your awareness about ID Theft, Spyware and Online "Friends." http://www.onguardonline.gov/games/overview.aspx

Media-Savvy Kids by Meg Lundstrom

For students inundated by images, critical thinking skills help sort fact from fiction

http://teacher.scholastic.com/products/instructor/nov04_mediasavvy.htm

The web site contains a list of additional resources about media awareness and education.

Chapter 10

Passwords, the Front Line of Defense

How to create secure passwords

Passwords are a necessary component of our lives today. We use them for access to online banking, credit cards, gaming, mutual fund, college savings and retirement accounts, just to name a few. They are also the most vulnerable link in our online armor because we often create poor passwords, leave them where they can easily be found or allow them to be phished or captured by key loggers.

Today, there are programs in use that are specifically designed to crack into people's online accounts by the brute force of repeated guessing. These programs are capable of trying every word in the English dictionary, as well as dictionaries of many foreign languages, in their effort to break into an account. They search words spelled backwards. Some will try common word combinations or words with numbers attached such as school222. These programs can test millions of passwords in a few minutes.

Passwords are also often picked up because we don't exercise safe Internet behavior. For example, it is never wise to access private password-protected accounts from public computers such as those found in a hotel business center for guests, or at a conference center. Additionally, hackers can use programs to capture passwords in publicly available wireless networks unless our computers are equipped with excellent methods of encryption.

Also, most people use the same password for all their personal accounts. This is certainly understandable when we all must keep track of PIN numbers on a variety of cards, home telephone numbers, multiple family cell phone numbers, social security numbers as well as passwords. But scammers depend on this weakness, which explains why they try to phish our password to our social networks or personal blogs, and then use them to try to gain access to our banks and credit card accounts.

Often, the reason our passwords are "cracked" is simply because they are so easily guessed. Nationally, the most commonly used passwords are:

1. Names of baseball, football or basketball teams.

2. Birth dates of a family member.

3. The year of a special sports event such as the year the Chicago Cubs won the World Series. 1908.

4. The word "password" or a variation such as "password1" or password spelled backwards.

5. The number sequence "123456" or letter/number variation such as "abc123" or "123abc."

6. The name of a family member, pet, favorite TV show character, celebrity or band.

Here are several tips to reduce the chances that your passwords will be compromised:

1. Never log in to a password-protected website from a public computer.

2. When you do log in to a password-protected web site, never allow your web browser to save your password. Some spyware can "suck" private information, including passwords, right out of a web browser.

3. Check that the wireless device you use to connect to the Internet, such as a laptop, is connecting with the latest security standards. Don't assume that it is! The easiest way to check this is to bring your laptop to the store where you bought it (or most any computer store) and ask them to check it for you and tell you what standard protocol your laptop uses. [For example, WEP encryption is no longer considered a good choice.]

4. Never leave your password on a piece of paper near your computer. If you want to write it down, keep it far away from your computer. You might consider putting half of it one location and the other half in another. You might even consider changing one character so that, even if found, the password won't work. [Of course you will have to remember the character that was changed.]

5. Never use any personal information to create a password (such as the names and birthdays of any family member or pets).

6. ONLY use secure passwords!

How to create secure passwords:

There are a few simple guidelines that you can use to create VERY STRONG passwords that are extremely difficult to crack but not too difficult to remember. They are:

1. Always use a mix of letters and numbers.

2. Use a mix of UPPER- and lowercase letters. (Passwords are case-sensitive!)

3. Use characters that are not letters or numbers such as **=**
! $ #.

(Many web sites won't allow punctuation to be used in the creation of passwords; you will have to experiment to find out what non-letter, non-number characters are allowed.)

4. Create acronyms from a poem, song or favorite quote/expression.

5. Always use a password that contains at least eight characters.

For example:

The first five words of the United States National Anthem are, "Oh, say can you see."

Use these words to create the acronym "oscys."

Add two numbers that mean something to you such as your grandmother's street address.

Play with UPPER and lower case, substitute $ for S, and add an = to create

32=oCy

Other good examples include:

!mYdoG8it=   from "My dog ate it"

iPa2tfotU$ from "I pledge allegiance to the flag of the United States"

aNwycCdfY   from "Ask not what your country can do for you"

Try the following exercises to help you create a more secure password.

Creating a secure password 1:

1. Think of a line from a song and write it down.

2. Create an acronym from the first letter of each word in the line.

3. Change at least one letter (not the first!) to a capital letter.

4. Add a non-number, non-letter character, or substitute a ! for an i, $ for an s.

5. Add a two- or three-digit number that has some personal significance.

Creating a secure password 2:

1. Think of the name of someone you admire and write it down.

2. Create a four-letter acronym from the first two letters of their first and last names.

3. Change at least one letter (not the first!) to a capital letter.

4. Add a non-number, non-letter character or substitute a ! for an i, $ for an s.

5. Mix in two numbers taken from your age. Don't put these numbers next to each other.

Test your password:

How good is a password? Test your own personal passwords, or a password you are thinking of using, at this secure web site at Cornell University. Visit:

https://netidadmin.cit.cornell.edu/NetIDManagement/Passwor dCheck

How to create multiple passwords that you can remember for different accounts:

It is easier than you think to create a variety of passwords for different accounts. After you've made a good password using the techniques described above, simply modify one character multiple times. Here is an example.

Take the sentence "This is the password I use for my bank."

Make an acronym by taking the first letter of each word: **titpi-ufmb**

Change both letters "i" to an exclamation point; substitute a number 4 for the word "for" and then capitalize the first and last letters: **T!tp!u4mB**

Now substitute any word for the word bank and change the last letter accordingly:

Mutual fund **T!tp!u4mM**

Credit card **T!tp!u4mC**

Home log-in **T!tp!u4mH**

Someone else's account such as a daughter named Chelsea:

"This is the password I use for Chelsea's Savings"
T!tp!u4CS

One final important note:

Phishers (people who try to trick you into revealing various account log-in information) actually depend on a percentage of parents to use their child's name and birth dates to create their passwords to their financial accounts. At least since early in 2007, phishers have tricked teens into letting them into their "private" social networks such as Facebook or MySpace. Once on the inside, the phishers used programs to collect the personal information posted by everyone in that network. This typically includes names, birth dates and geographical location as many teens post all or some of this information. The phishers then use the information they have gathered to try and log in to major online banking and credit card accounts or banking accounts located in the geographical area of the person who was phished. They use other programs to automate these attempts, making it very easy for them. And it works in a small percentage of accounts.

Chapter Resources:

Krebs, Brian. (January 15, 2007)

Note to MySpace Users: Get Better Passwords, Washington-Post.com

http://blog.washingtonpost.com/securityfix/2007/01/myspace_phishers_hook_hundreds.html

Evers, Joris. (December 15, 2006)
Report: Net Users Picking Safer Passwords, ZDNet News.com
http://news.zdnet.com/2100-1009_22-6144312.html

Scalet, Sarah D. (December 1, 2005)
How to Write Better Passwords, CSOonline.com
http://www.csoonline.com/read/120105/ht_passwords.html

No author cited. (November 2, 2005)
Powerful Passwords, PCMag.com
http://www.pcmag.com/article2/0,1895,1880305,00.asp

Granger, Sarah (January 17, 2002)
The Simplest Security: A Guide To Better Password Practices, SecurityFocus.com
http://www.securityfocus.com/infocus/1537

No author cited. (April, 1997)
Password Security: A Guide for Students, Faculty, and Staff of the University of Michigan, University of Michigan, Information Technology Division, Reference R1192

http://www.umich.edu/~policies/pw-security.html

Chapter 11

Fraud and Phishing

How to recognize and avoid scams and threats to your computer

"It has become appallingly obvious that our technology has exceeded our humanity."

~ Albert Einstein

Internet scams and threats come in all shapes and sizes. They come to you on the web, in advertisements, through social network ads and fake member pages, via pop-ups, emails, instant messages, in "free" software and even hidden inside images and downloaded music files. They are even turning up in cell phone text messages. In many cases, they affect PC and Mac users alike because many don't involve computer-specific downloaded software. One of the most successful types of scams perpetrated across the Internet is the phishing scam. Phishing is a scam in which the phisher tricks someone into revealing their username and password to sites that have value to the phisher. This includes banks, mutual fund accounts, credit card accounts, social networks (they are treasure troves of personal information) and even gaming sites. (Virtual game items such as characters, weapons and other resources can be sold online for real money.) It is fair to say that nearly every bank in the United States has been targeted by phishers and that the volume of phishing emails sent around the globe in a month exceeds one billion! (Anti-Phishing Working Group, Antiphishing.org; May, 2007)

We hope to raise your awareness and educate you how to spot and avoid the wide variety of Internet scams by showing samples here, explaining how many operate and giving you strategies for reducing your risk of being targeted, as well as how to teach your children.

Let's go phishing:

Well-known financial services such as Chase Bank, Bank of America and Paypal are heavily targeted by phishers. In the JP Morgan Chase Bank scam on the next page, the email recipient is told that new security measures require the recipient to log in to their account and a clickable link is conveniently provided. Phishing scams will offer up lots of different reasons why the recipient of the email must log in. Sometimes, the recipient is told the institution is conducting an audit, running maintenance or simply needs to verify user information. Whatever the reason, the email attempts to trick the recipient to click the link provided and then enter their log-in information. If the scammer is very sophisticated, not only will the link take the victim to a web site that appears exactly like their bank or credit card company, but after they enter their ID and password, they will actually be forwarded into their real account. Of course, their ID and password will have been captured by the phishers, to be used later. By forwarding the victim to the real site, the victim is unaware that they have been scammed.

What follows are three examples of phishing scams.

Note: This is a service message regarding the Chase Online Form.

Dear customer:

As part of the new security measures, all Chase bank customers are required to complete Chase Online Form. Please complete the form as soon as possible.

To access the form please click on the following link:

Chase Online Form

Thank you for being a valued customer.

Sincerely,

Online Banking Team

==

ATTENTION TO ALL CAPITAL ONE BANK CUSTOMERS

NECESSARY CRITICAL UPDATE

A critical update is available to remove unacceptable symbols from the wire submission page that is included with Capital One Bank Treasury Optimizer.

Critical Updates are intended to fix potential security risks in Business Objects Capital One Bank products.

These updates are highly recommended to ensure the security of Capital One Bank products.

For additional information about the latest service pack for Windows, click the following link to view the article in the Capital One Update Base:

To start update press **NEXT>>**

2008 Capital One Services, Inc.

===

Customer Support Center - Account Maintenance

Case ID Number: AT-09GP98-10-D709

Amazon.com Inc. is committed to maintaining a safe environment
for its community of buyers and sellers. To protect the security
of your account Amazon.com Inc. some of the advanced security
systems in the world and our anti-fraud teams regularly screen
the Amazon.com Inc. system for unusual activity.
In accordance with Amazon.com Inc.'s User Agreement and to ensure
that your account has not been compromised, access to your account was
limited. Your account access will remain limited until this issue has
been resolved. In order to secure your account and quickly restore
full access, we may require some specific information from you for the
following reason: we encourage you to log in and restore full access
as soon as possible. Please follow the link and renew your account information:

https://www.amazon.com/gp/rsl/ref=UTF8&login_viewRSL=1&rslpage=1

Completing all items will automatically restore your account access.

Thanks for your patience as we work together to protect your account.

Regards,
Customer Support Center.

Copyright 1996-2007, Amazon.com, Inc. or its affiliates

There are several ways to evaluate whether or not an email you've received is a phishing attempt:

1. Do you find misspelled words or incorrect grammar in the email? English is a second language for many phishers and it shows in their construction of the email. However, a grammatically correct, well-written email does not mean that it is legitimate!

2. Web browser detection of phishing sites has improved markedly. The latest version of Internet Explorer and Firefox, for example, will notify you when you visit web sites that are suspected forgeries.

3. Another way to determine that an email is fraudulent is to hover your mouse over the clickable link found in the email. Look CAREFULLY at the URL (web address) that displays at the bottom of the web browser window. Is the domain that of your trusted website? Don't be fooled!

www.chaseonline.chase.com is not the same as

www.chaseonline.chase.com.hgtrk.co.uk

www.paypal.com is not the same as www.paypa1.com or

www.paypai.com

www.capitalonebank.com is not the same as

top.capitalonebank.compub.login.htmlbank.serv.manager

4. Consider the content of the email itself. Financial services will never ask you to verify who you are via email or ask you to log in to check that your account is working. If there is ever any doubt about the authenticity of an email, call your financial institution and inquire.

Nigerian Advance-Fee Scam

This is one of the oldest, and most successful, Internet scams. The "Nigerian advance-fee scam," has successfully duped thousands of people around the world out of many millions of dollars. Even bankers, lawyers and other educated and professional people have been fooled.

This scam's history and success is detailed at www.crimes-of-persuasion.com/Crimes/Business/nigerian.htm. Because this scam first began in the late 1990s, thousands of variations have evolved and pour into people's email inboxes daily. Some variations of this scam have become extremely sophisticated and appear very legitimate. Here are two examples:

==

Subject: hello

From: "Themba Lindani" <absathemba@gmail.com>

Dear Friend,

I am Mr. Themba Lindani, Auditor, foreign remittance department Absa Bank Admin, and asking for your indulgence in re-profiling funds, which we want to transfer to a foriegn account. The full amount to be transferred is ($14,700,000). I am only contacting you as a foreigner because this fund cannot be approved to a local Bank here in South Africa, and the funds are in US Dollars. The owner of this account is Mr. Morris Thompson from America, and he died since 2000 in an air crash along with his wife & Daughter on 31/01/2000 in an Alaska Airlines Flight 261 with other passengers on board. You can confirm this from http://www.cnn.com/2000/US/02/01/alaska.airlines.list/

I am proposing 30% for you for your assistance while my colleagues and I will receive 60%, and 10% earmarked for purposes of expenses. Should you be interested in this business transaction, which I sincerely appreciate and hope that you will, kindly provid me with the below information:

(1) Your personal telephone number

(2) fax number

(3) Full Names

(4) age

(5) company, if any

(6) Residential Address

We do not want these money to go into a government account as unclaimed bills, hence, some officials and I, want you to present yourself as the next of kin in relation with the deceased, so the funds can be remitted into your account. On receipt of your acceptance and the above informations., you will be communicated with the exact steps to take, to enable us conclude this transaction urgently and confidentially. Please reply me on my confidential email on themba.lindani@gmail.com

Best Regards

Mr. Themba Lindani

==

Dear Beloved in Christ,

I am Mrs. Mary Parker, suffering from cancerous ailment. I am married to Mr. Robert Parker, my husband worked with Chevron/Texaco in the United Kingdom for twenty years before he died in the year 2003. My late husband deposited the sum of £ 17.5 Million (Seventeen Million Five Hundred Thousand Pounds) with a Bank in United Kingdom. Recently, my Doctor told me that I have limited days to live due to the stroke and cancerous problems I am suffering from. I have decided to donate this fund to you and want you to use this gift which comes from my husbands effort to fund the upkeep of widows and charities worldwide. I took this decision because I do not have any child that will inherit this money and my husband relatives are bourgeois and very wealthy persons and I do not want my husband hard earned money to be misused. Awaiting your urgent reply via my email.address:maryparkers_07@yahoo.co.uk

With God all things are possible.

Your Sister in Christ,

Mrs. Mary Parker

The object of the scam is to convince the victim to either send money in advance in order to receive a huge payout, or to trick the victim into revealing enough bank account and routing information to enable the scammers to gain direct access to that account. These scams have expanded into stocks as well as cash accounts and have often used scare tactics and threats to intimidate their victims.

The value of information:

One of the reasons that children and teens do not understand the risks they routinely take online is because they don't understand the value of information. This is especially true of personal information. They aren't aware of damage caused by identity theft or impersonation. Combined with the fact that online privacy is an illusion, it has become impossibly difficult for anyone with a digital life to make him or herself truly free from identity theft. However, some of us willingly give away our personal information. We do this when we create accounts to web sites, set up online email, sign up with marketers/vendors or respond to queries for things of interest. The email that follows is a simple example of the thousands sent daily that are fishing for information.

From: carlson@gornotrans.com

Subject: part time jobs

Sir/Madam

REGIONAL PAYMENT RECEIVING AGENT NEEDED

DT-systems Ltd. is based in Lithuania. We specialize in exportation and importation. We export our products to North America, South America, Eastern and Western Europe and Southern Asia.

We are looking for a payment representative in UK, USA and Canada. Salary is 10% of every payment you receive on our behalf. All charges such as tax and fees will be deducted from the balance 90%.

For this job position you have to provide with your bank account information. Note: Even if you have a real job, you can be part of our business anyway as your regular and part-time job can be easily combined, your work for our company will not disturb your regular work.

If you are interested in this opportuni1y please send out your contact information to our company email:

1) Your Full names:

2) Your Address and Postal code:

3) Home/office phone number and cell phone number:

4) Occupation and Sex:

Your address should be correct and complete (including your state and country) because you will also be receiving cheques to your address.

Attention ! Please write only to this email : tupn153btgc@gmail.com

Managers of our company will come in contact with you as soon as possible. Having received the information, we will give you a contract, in which the responsibility of both sides is fixed.

Sincerely, Jonas Varnas

HR manager

You might recognize this as another variation of the Nigerian Advance-Fee Scam. Note the personal information that the victim is also asked to give up in just the first email. You should never provide this kind of information to anyone over the Internet, especially to solicitations from unknown sources. Many readers may feel self-assured after looking at the examples provided because they may seem like obvious scams to which they would never fall prey. However, many scams are disguised to look like official government announcements or links to news articles about current events.

From: United States District Court [subpoena@uscourts.com]
Sent: Monday, April 14, 2008 7:30 AM
To: John Doe
Subject: Subpoena in case #44-357-DKH

AO 88(Rev.11/94) Subpoena in a Civil Case

Issued by the
UNITED STATES DISTRICT COURT

Issued to: John Doe
ABC Company
(415)123-4567

SUBPOENA IN A CIVIL CASE

Case number: 44-357-DKH
United States
District Court

SAMPLE FRAUDULENT EMAIL

YOU ARE HEREBY COMMANDED to appear and testify before the Grand Jury of the United States District Court at the place, date, and time specifiied below

Place: United States Courthouse Date and Time: May 7, 2008
880 Front Street   9:00 a.m. PST
San Diego, California
92101

Room: Grand Jury Room
room 5217

Issuing officers name and address: O'Mevely & Meyers LLP; 400 South Hope Street, Los Angeles, CA 90071

Please download the entire document on this matter(follow this link) and print it for your record

This subpoena shall remain in effect until you are granted leave to depart by the court or by an officer on behalf of the court.

From: xlyh@capto-nd.com

Subject: Destruction in China continues

Deadly earthquake shook China again

http://118.38.187.xxx/

Both of the previous email scams direct the intended victim to click a link or visit a web site. However, visiting the web site would result in the installation of a worm virus containing a key logger that captures everything the victim types on the keyboard, including passwords, and sends the information to the scammers.

Scams are now pouring into our cell phones via texting. This is called "vishing" and can have just as deadly consequences. Cell phones with full Internet access or that receive email are vulnerable to both web-based and text-based scams. "Spear-phishing" is a new phenomenon in which the scammer acquires small amounts of personal information about an individual and then uses it to craft a personal email scam to that individual. Such emails with real personal information are much more "authoritative" and convincing. That is one of the reasons why scammers target teen's social networks. They easily trick teens into letting them into their networks. Once on the inside, they use programs like the Fox Adder to suck up lots of personal information from the entire network of friends.

This chapter can't possibly expose all of the various types of scams that target us on the Internet and through telecommunications technology. Hopefully, you get the idea. Yet there are things that we can do to reduce our risks of falling prey to scams. We need to teach our children these rules for their life in the digital world too. They are also targeted heavily in every online venue.

Methods for avoiding scams:

1. Never click links in emails. If you truly believe the authenticity of an email, don't click the embedded link. Instead, open your web browser and type in the address or look up the address yourself in Google.

2. Verify the email you receive. Again, if you believe the authenticity of an email, call your financial institution to verify it.

3. Look carefully at emails you receive. Does the sender's email address match the address you are told to contact? Is the sender's address from the exact official domain of the institution? Does the sender's name match the name found in the email address? Is a complete address and telephone number provided? If the answer to any of these questions is no, the email is likely part of a scam.

4. Learn how to determine who actually owns a domain. It's easy. Simply visit a "Who Is" web directory. There are hundreds of them on the Internet. Enter "Who is" (with quotes around it) into the Google search field to return many "Whois" directories such as Whois.net, Whois.sc and Whois.domaintools.com. In the search field of a Whois directory, enter the exact domain name or string of numbers (IP Address) and click Go. (Enter the verify code if you are asked for one.) For example, when I hover my mouse over the embedded link in the JP Morgan Chase Bank phishing email, the real Internet address is revealed at the bottom of the email as:

chaseonline.chase.com.hgtrk.org.uk

A WhoIs look-up of this domain returns error messages. The WhoIs look-up should have confirmed that the domain is owned by Chase Bank.

5. Use the power of Google. Google has the power of demonstrating a kind of collective intelligence. Copy the exact name of the web site to which an embedded link points, or take an interesting or unique phrase from the body of an email. Paste it into Google's search field and put quotes around it. Quotes tell Google to search for exactly those words in exactly that order. Click search. **Chaseonline.chase.com.hgtrk.org.uk**, Google returned several links, all of which addressed phishing

scams. Enter the phrase "This is a service message regarding the Chase Online Form" in quotes and the first six links are about phishing scams and spam email.

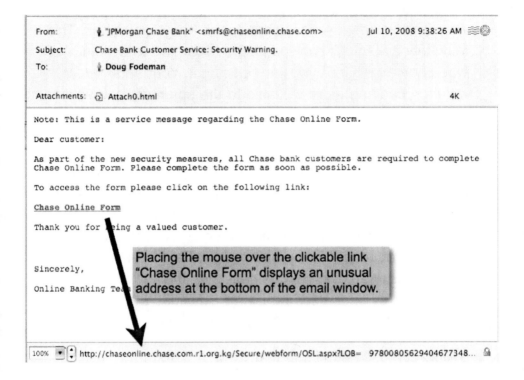

Note: This is a service message regarding the Chase Online Form.

Dear customer:

As part of the new security measures, all Chase bank customers are required to complete Chase Online Form. Please complete the form as soon as possible.

To access the form please click on the following link:

Chase Online Form

Thank you for being a valued customer.

Sincerely,

Online Banking Team

Placing the mouse over the clickable link "Chase Online Form" displays an unusual address at the bottom of the email window.

100%   http://chaseonline.chase.com.r1.org.kg/Secure/webform/OSL.aspx?LOB= 97800805629404677348...

6. Never, EVER, give out your personal email address to anyone other than your trusted friends and family. Use a "disposable" email account to give to businesses, marketers, online forms and web sites. Disposable accounts are free and easy to set up. Visit Gmail.com or Yahoo.com to create an account in just a couple of minutes. However, remember that when you set up your disposable accounts, don't provide real personal information there either! Use these "throwaway" email addresses when you need an email address and want to protect the privacy of your personal and most-used email address. Unused email accounts at these free services will simply expire after a period of time due to non-activity. To read a review of free email services, visit:

email.about.com/od/freeemailreviews/tp/free_email.htm.

7. Never respond to suspicious email. Delete suspicious email WITHOUT opening them first. Many spam email contain small amounts of computer code called a **web beacon**. The web beacon actually reports back to the spammer that an email was opened, when it was opened, and how many times. This information is valuable to spammers because it tells them what type of email will trick you into opening it. Your email address will then become more valuable to the spammer and sold to other spammers for a higher price because you have demonstrated a willingness to look at what they are offering.

8. Don't do business with anyone whom you cannot verify via an alternate source. You can certainly trust Amazon.com or Gap.com enough to do business with them online. However, do not do business with a name you don't recognize, can't find a telephone number for or information about through a Better Business Bureau. Call the business over the phone, verify the address or even contact the Better Business Bureau in their city to determine the authenticity of the business.

9. If it seems too good to be true, it is.

10. NEVER be scared or intimidated by someone or something because they sound "official" or appear to be an authority. Scams have been sent in the name of the FBI, Justice Department, Internet Crime Complaint Center, IRS and various health insurers, just to name a few. Spear-phishing attempts may include first and last names, city and street information or even information about family members to make them appear legitimate.

11. In today's digital world it is impossible to control the flow, release or use of information about us. Everyone from summer camps our children attend to health insurers or even our pet's veterinarians, have personal information about us. Anywhere we use a credit or ATM card we leave digital footprints. Our

very search behavior online tells Google or some other service a great deal about us. One way you can make it difficult for anyone to open accounts in your name, or your child's name, is to request a fraud alert on your credit account. Visit any one of the three major credit reporting agencies listed here and request a fraud alert be placed on your account. Each company is required to contact the other two companies. The alert will not last forever but can be renewed. In addition, you have the right to receive a free credit report once each year. Request this for both you and your spouse.

Credit Reporting Companies:

www.Experian.com

www.Transunion.com

www.Equifax.com

Cramming, cell phone bills gone bad:

Cramming refers to a telephone company placing unauthorized, fraudulent or deceptive charges on your telephone bill. It happens quite frequently and has been reported by cell phone users from every major cell phone carrier. To read some of the stories posted by people across the United States, visit http://www.jamsterscam.com.

Look at several months of your family's cell phone bill and review the charges. Do you see any "generic" charges listed simply as "download", "data" or "premium services" without any explanation? Call the phone service and ask them to explain these charges. Ask them to identify the "3rd party company" that is actually billing you through your cell phone carrier's bill. Ask your family if anyone had actually ordered those services. If no one did, you've been crammed! Ask the phone company to remove the charges!

Identity theft:

Identity theft occurs when someone obtains/steals and uses your personal information to pretend to be you online. They may log in to one of your personal accounts or by finding out enough information about you to open up accounts in your name. When perpetrated against adults, the motivation is typically for financial gain. However, identity theft is rampant amongst children and teens, too. The reasons, however, are predominantly to harass, embarrass, humiliate or hurt the child/teen. It is so widespread because, all too often, younger children share their passwords with others. Older children are likely to select passwords that are easily cracked or guessed by people who know them. The reason that identity theft of children and teens is primarily for the purpose of harassment is because children/teens spend so much of their time creating, nurturing, and building their play and social worlds online. Thus the Internet has increasingly become the weapon of choice for purely malicious behavior by others who are intent on causing pain, hurt or embarrassment.

Take the Identity Theft PC Perfect Information Safety Quiz posted at the Identity Theft Resource Center and calculate your quiz score. Visit:

www.idtheftcenter.org/artman2/publish/c_theft_test/Fact_She et_118_PC_Perfect_-_information_Safety_Quiz.shtml

A shorter alternative quiz to evaluate online risks for identity theft is provided by TDBankNorth. Visit: www.tdbanknorth. com/bank/onlinerisks1.aspx

For additional information you can visit the Identity Theft Resource Center (idtheftcenter.org/) and click on "Scams and Consumer Alerts."

Teach your child the most common causes of identity theft and how to avoid them:

1. Children give out their passwords to their friends who, in turn, may give it to others!

2. Someone sees a child enter his/her password. ("Over the shoulder" theft is easily perpetrated because children typically don't consider or respect the privacy of others.)

3. Children don't log off properly from a computer, thereby allowing someone to jump onto their account after them. Don't just close a window when done. Quit the application and log off the computer.

4. Children leave "selected" a check-box such as "Remember my password."

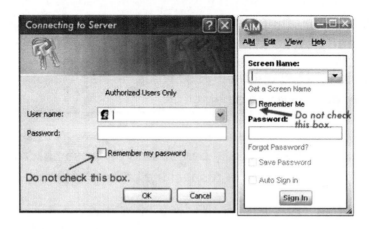

5. Children use passwords that are very easy to crack by others who know them or use a password cracker.

6. Like many adults, children may leave a password written on paper near their computers or in their notebooks.

7. Key loggers, spyware or other hacker applications on a computer may capture a password. This includes passwords that are saved into a web browser. Never allow passwords to be saved in web browsers.

8. Children may be tricked into entering passwords into phishing sites such as fake MySpace or Facebook pages.

Chapter Resources:

Anti-Phishing Working Group
www.antiphishing.org/

FBI Internet Fraud
www.fbi.gov/majcases/fraud/internetschemes.htm

Fighting Back Against Identity Theft from the Federal Trade Commission
www.ftc.gov/bcp/edu/microsites/idtheft/

Identity Theft Prevention and Survival
www.identitytheft.org/

Identity Theft Resource Center - Blog Sense (Fact Sheet 127)
www.idtheftcenter.org/artman2/publish/t_facts/Fact_Sheet_12
7.shtml

Identity Theft Resource Center - Teen Resources
www.idtheftcenter.org/teen/teen.html

Internet Crime Complaint Center
www.ic3.gov

Preventing Identity Theft Online - Tips from TDBankNorth
www.tdbanknorth.com/bank/preventingidtheft_online.html

Spam Scams
www.spamscams.net/

"It helps me remember that when I'm online, nothing I do is really private."

Illustration by David Saunders www.DavidThomasSaunders.com

Chapter 12

Privacy Online – an Oxymoron
How to better protect your family's online privacy

Online privacy is an illusion. Even sites that require us to enter our passwords and an ID can be compromised. There are dozens of ways in which our privacy online is eroded daily. Here are some examples:

1. We give our email address, along with personal information, to legitimate stores who sell it to others. Even traditional "brick-and-mortar" stores may do this. It may be transferred or sold many times over and our inbox soon feels the consequences of that spread.

2. Security flaws in software are routinely discovered and a download fix is required to repair the flaw. They are often discovered only when a security breach occurs. Hacks have been found in virtually every form of software over the years and hackers do their very best to exploit these insecurities for their own personal and financial gain.

3. We are tricked into revealing our personal information. Phishing attempts now number in the billions monthly. Publicly available computers may harbor clandestinely installed key loggers that record every user's keystroke and send them back to the hacker.

4. We are besieged by scammers' emails that try to trick us into visiting web sites in which our computers are hit by "drive-by downloads." Unbeknownst to us, software is downloaded that causes the installation of additional hacking software (spyware, adware or other malware) that monitors our online activities, steals our personal data and subverts our computer's resources for someone else's illegal use.

5. Online giants such as Google and Facebook analyze our online behavior, package those statistics, along with our account information, and sell it to marketers.

6. Our own lack of knowledge puts us at risk. We may enter credit card information in a web site that does not use acceptable standard security protocols because we don't know how to recognize when these protocols are in place or missing. We may send personal data across the Internet in "clear text" that can easily be copied and read.

7. Many online communities, such as social networks, create a false sense of security because they have log-in pages. Not only are such log-in screens hacked, phished and users tricked into letting scammers on the inside, but once on the inside, scammers use a variety of tools to search for and copy personal data found throughout the community of users.

8. Web sites we visit may place data mining cookies in our web browsers that track our online behavior. That behavior is then reported to marketers who then target us with ads based on our behavior.

9. Businesses that keep our personal information are under threat by hackers daily. If you watch the news about such events, you know that they sometimes lose the battle and our personal information is stolen.

10. Legitimate advertisers and scammers alike may use web beacons, also called web bugs and clear GIFs, to determine which emails we open and how many times we look at them. A web beacon usually consists of a very small transparent graphic image that is placed in an email. A web beacon allows the email sender to record some simple actions of the email recipient. Web beacons can also be used on web pages to track web site behavior.

How private is your online life?

There is simply no online privacy. And the more we live our lives online, the easier it becomes to find out information about us. Look for yourself. Try these very easy "low level" tests to see how easy it is to discover information about you or your family.

1. Visit Google.com and enter your name in quotes. (Try entering the names of other family members as well.) Quotes tell Google to find exactly those words in that order.

2. What do others reveal about you? Visit www.jigsaw.com

Jigsaw is an example of a website in which visitors are given rewards, points in this case, by giving up information on others. At one point Jigsaw.com actually paid out cash for information. Are you in their database? You can read more about the invasion of our privacy online by visiting Time.com's article "Online Snooping Gets Creepy" at

www.time.com/time/business/article/0,8599,1649121,00.html

Web sites such as PeekYou.com, Pipl.com, and Spock.com make it easy to scour the web for information about you.

3. What does your telephone number reveal about you? Again, visit Google.com and enter your telephone number into the search field with area code and dashes. Click search. Many of us will discover that Google will return our names, address and a map with directions to our house. If you wish to have this information removed, click the "Phonebook Results" and look for a link to have this information removed. Try entering the phone numbers of friends and other family members. Unfortunately, there are many other online services that can also provide this information. Visit each of the web sites below and try searching for your own name or your spouse's name.

http://switchboard.intelius.com

To request that your information be removed from the Switchboard database, click the "Privacy" link at the bottom of the main page and then follow the Opt-Out link.

http://www.anywho.com

To request that your information be removed from the AnyWho database, click the "Help" link at the bottom of the main page and then follow the link "How to remove your residential listing."

4. Visit Zillow.com and enter your street, city, state and zip code. Zillow contains a great deal of information about our homes and their value. At the time of publication there is no way to formerly request that your information be removed from the Zillow database.

5. View a sampling of advertising cookies that may be in your computer and monitoring your browsing behavior. Visit the Network Advertising Initiative online (http://www.networkadvertising. org/) and click their Consumer Opt-Out tool in order to find a partial list of web browser cookies that are monitoring your online activity. This tool will only detect a small percent of the possible cookies you may have monitoring your online activity. Though you have the option to opt-out of these advertising cookies, there may be many other cookies placed in your computer that you cannot opt-out of. It is best to set your browser NOT to accept third-party cookies. Third-party cookies are those that come from a web site other than the one you are on. (See tips list below.)

6. It is possible today to say anything about anyone on the Internet and that information can be sent around the web. Sites like JuicyCampus.com encouraged innuendo, rumors and gossip about college students. Read "College gossip site

totally busted. Insults about looks, race and sexual history are 'just the tip of the iceberg'" by Brad Haynes. Updated March 20, 2008.

http://www.msnbc.msn.com/id/23705921/

There are many such sites:

GossipReport.com   TheDirty.com

RottenNeighbor.com   DontDateHimGirl.com

Note: In February, 2009 JuicyCampus.com closed and its domain points to College Anonymous Confession Board, or CollegeACB.com.

By now, you get the point about online privacy. There are, however, many things that can be done to reduce the erosion of your privacy and reduce the risks that come from such loss of privacy. These risks include being victimized by scammers, identity theft, fraud and having our real-life reputations damaged.

Tips for protecting your online privacy:

1. Do not sign up to receive email notifications by web sites for offers and updates. Even if you trust the web site, you have no control over what they do with your personal information or to whom they may sell it. If you truly wish to receive email notification, subscriptions or such, create a disposable email address with a service like Gmail or Yahoo. They are free and take just a couple of minutes to create.

2. When using computers that are not yours, avoid going to web sites that require you to enter your personal information, especially log-in ID and password. Never use "publically-available" computers to access banking or credit card accounts.

3. When you enter your log-in ID and password to enter a web site, do not allow the web browser to auto-save this information for future log-ins. Remember, some spyware can read these fields and send the data to hackers.

4. Do not use the auto-fill (auto-forms) feature of any web browser.

5. Protect the privacy of your personal email address. Use it for your trusted friends and family. If a business or online form asks you for an email address, use the disposable address you created at Yahoo.com or Gmail.com.

6. Never publish your private email address on web sites or in online discussion groups. Spambots routinely harvest email addresses from online forums and discussion groups.

7. Don't fall prey to the hundreds of pop-ups and advertisements offering free items or claiming that you have won a prize. In order to determine if you have won anything at all, these pop-ups/ads will require you to enter more and more personal private information. Ultimately, the vast majority of users never receive anything of value in return.

8. Set your web browser to block "third-party" cookies. These are cookies that come from web sites other than the site you are currently visiting. Access to your web browser's cookies can be found in the browser preferences. Launch your web browser and look through the menu bar items for something called Preferences.

9. Explore the privacy and security settings of your web browser. Turn those settings on as high as you can tolerate. Sometimes high settings may make it difficult to visit certain web sites so you may have to experiment. But things like blocking pop-ups, deleting cookies, clearing history or per-

sonal information and preventing sites from installing add-ons is easily done and is worthwhile.

A note about cookies:

Not all cookies are bad and not all cookies are data miners attempting to track your online activities. For example, some may store a visitor's selected preferences for using a particular web site such as telling Google to try to remove adult content from returned searches. For those of you who wish to have a closer look at the cookies that get installed on your computer in order to manage them, there are many programs available. Visit Download.com and enter the search term "cookie." Look at the user ratings to see what others might recommend. If you use Firefox for your web browser there are many add-ons that can help you track and remove cookies as well as reduce the advertising that appears on your web pages. Visit Mozilla.com and click the link for Add-Ons.

10. Create and use secure passwords that are at least eight characters long. (See Chapter 10 on passwords.) It would be best to create a set of related passwords so that you don't use the same single password for all your online business.

11. NEVER enter private information online such as credit card, social security or other financial account information unless you know you are using a secure web site. To determine if a web site is using a secure protocol to transfer information there are two things to look for. In the navigation bar at the top of all web browsers, the URL (web address) is displayed and typically begins with **http://**. For a secure transaction, the URL should begin with **https://** and the "s" stands for "secure." Also, in the lower-right corner of the WEB BROWSER WINDOW, look for a lock symbol. For example, Amazon.com's lock symbol looks like this:

Many phishers try to trick people by showing a lock symbol on the actual web page instead of on the wall of the browser itself. Don't be duped! NEVER log in or purchase from a web site if you do not see the HTTPS protocol in the address bar AND the lock symbol in the lower right corner of the web browser. **Exception:** Some web sites, such as Facebook, hide the https protocol from view even though it is in use. Look at the screen shot of the Facebook log-in page:

It appears to ask the user to log in from an HTTP connection. However, if one clicks the log-in button without entering any information, the web address immediately changes to the following, which shows that the actual log-in is via HTTPS.

12. Check before installing "free" software. "Free" often has a price. Many free items on the Internet many actually contain adware or spyware. If there is software you would like to download and install, first search Google for the name of the item. Include words like adware, spyware and malware in your

search. Does Google return links that raise any red flags or concerns? If so, don't install it!

A special note about Apple computers:

Until June 2008, there was never any spyware or adware found to install on the Mac operating system and there have only been very few viruses as well. However, in June, three Trojan horses were discovered that install spyware. Still, this number of software threats against the Mac operating system is tiny when compared to the millions of various threats that plague PC users running the Windows operating system.

13. Run operating system and web browser updates and patches. This is true for both Mac and PC owners. Keep your computer and web browser software updated. Some web browsers such as Firefox will update automatically, just like the operating system.

14. It cannot be said enough: Install quality anti-virus and anti-spyware programs and make sure your subscriptions are up-to-date so the definitions are maintained. There are many quality anti-virus products such as those by Symantec, Norton and Sophos. It is harder, though, to find quality anti-spyware software. Much of it is ineffective and some of it is actually spyware or extortion-ware disguised as anti-spyware software. (Extortion-ware is a type of malware that notifies the users that there is some type of virus or other threat on their computer. A link is provided to a web site where they may purchase a product to remove that virus or threat. The irony is that the malware still remains hidden and working on the user's computer even after the extortion has been paid.) Three decent products for the Windows operating system and free at the time of publication, are Windows Defender, Spybot and AdAware. It is not

uncommon to have two of them installed as no anti-spyware software has ever been found to be more than about 80% effective. For more information, visit www.spywarewarrior. com.

If you would like to watch a 12-minute online educational video about drive-by downloads and spyware that infect PCs from WatchGuard.com, visit:

http://video.google.com/videoplay?docid=-3351512772400238297

A drive-by download is a program that is automatically down-loaded and installed on a PC (not Apple's computers) without your knowledge or consent the moment you visit a web page. The downloaded application often directs the installation of more spyware and malware applications onto your PC, or it might turn your computer into a zombie and can even install key logging software that steals your passwords by recording exactly what you type on your keyboard.

Parents might find it interesting to know that Cory, the young man in the video behind the desk, began playing around with computers at a young age and experimented with computer code and applications in a way he shouldn't have. Much to his parents' surprise, the FBI showed up on his doorstep when he was 14 to talk to him about his hack-ing attempts! He has come a long way since then and now works for WatchGuard.com

Special warning about file-sharing software:

Remember Napster? After the Recording Industry Association of America successfully litigated it for the theft of music files, the concept of peer-to-peer (P2P) file sharing was reborn anew. Like the hydra whose head was cut off, what followed the successful litigation of Napster was the birth of many new P2P software. Grokster, Morpheus, Music City, Shareaza, BearShare and the most popular Limewire and KaZaA, were born. These file-sharing communities still share a great many files illegally but have been more difficult for the RIAA to shut down because of the way they share files. They work by turning all of our individual computers into little file-sharing servers, without any centralized server belonging to the software manufacturer. Teens are especially drawn to file-sharing software because of the tremendous amount of free, albeit mostly illegal, music files that can be found and downloaded. Besides the legal issues of pirating music files, there are several serious issues with P2P software.

1. Many of the files circulating on P2P networks have been found to contain Trojan horses, worms and viruses. Depending on which security agency is reporting on this problem, it has been estimated that 25% - 33% of the music shared through P2P software is infected.

2. P2P software is predicated on the idea of sharing files. Even if the majority of files are music files, there is a great deal of pornography as well.

3. Some of these programs have been found to install spyware and adware. SpywareWarrior's author, Professor Eric Howes, found KaZaA to install 35 different pieces of spyware, along with KaZaA in 2006. Ben Edelman, a respected spyware/adware researcher, found KaZaA 3.0 to install adware in addition to the KaZaA application in 2007. Limewire has never

been found to install adware or spyware as of the date of publication.

4. Even if your P2P software doesn't install any spyware, your family's privacy is at risk. By default, P2P software might be sharing the entire contents of your computer with other P2P users. Do your children have any of these programs installed on your computers? If so, check the application's preferences to see WHAT is being shared. Our recommendation is not to share anything. Turn sharing off. You may be allowing others to gain access to files located in your computer.

Chapter Resources:

Electronic Frontier Foundation (EFF.org)

EFF's Top 12 Ways to Protect Your Online Privacy; by Santon McCandlish, April 2002.

Visit: www.eff.org/wp/effs-top-12-ways-protect-your-online-privacy

Six Tips to Protect Your Search Privacy; September, 2006.Visit: www.eff.org/wp/six-tips-protect-your-search-privacy

GetNetWise.org

GetNetWise has information about protecting your computer, your privacy, your children, and even "How-To" videos on these and related topics.

GetSafeOnline.com

How to be anonymous

Visit: www.getsafeonline.org/nqcontent.cfm?a_id=1132

OnGuardOnline.com

The risks of P2P software are described at OnGuardOnline. Visit Onguardonline.gov/p2p.html.

Included on the site is a game quiz to test your knowledge about the risks of P2P software, as well as a video from iSafe about some of the issues associated with P2P software.

PrivacyRights.org

The Privacy Rights Clearinghouse posts a thorough list of data vendors who offer an "opt-out" policy and those who don't. Visit: www.privacyrights.org/ar/infobrokers.htm

W3.org

The World Wide Web Consortium has developed a Platform for Privacy Preferences project called P3P. Find out more about their recommendations and initiatives to build privacy tools into web browsers by visiting www.w3.org/P3P/

WorldPrivacyForum.org

The World Privacy Forum has posted the top ten "Opt-Outs" it recommends to consumers. Show your parent(s) or guardian(s) and recommend that they take advantage of this service. Visit: www.worldprivacyforum.org/toptenoptout.html

Chapter 13

Parental Control Software

Taking control of your family's Internet experiences

All parental control software generally falls into one of three categories:

- **Content filtering software**

- **Time limiting software**

- **Key logging software**

Content filters attempt to review the content of a web page and, depending on a child's filter settings, either block or allow the web page to be seen. Most quality products offer 15 to 25 different categories of web pages that parents can allow their child to see or be blocked, such as racism, pornography, online auctions, hacking, violence, gambling, social networking, etc.

Time limiting software attempts to do exactly what it sounds like, limit the hours in a day that a child can use the Internet or certain software on the Internet such as massive multi-player games like *World of Warcraft* or instant messaging client software. Some parents have asked us if we know of software that will allow Internet access or game-playing for a set amount of time per day and then shut down Internet or game-play after that accumulated limit is reached. Not too many products have this specific ability.

A **Key Logger** is software that will record every single keystroke that is made on a computer and report that back to the person who installed it, even by emailing log files every day.

This type of software is also used very successfully by scammers to capture personal information, such as online credit card/bank log-in IDs and passwords. That's one good reason why it is NEVER a good idea to access personal private accounts from public computers, such as in a hotel or at a conference, and why it is so important to have anti-spyware software installed on our home PCs. (Apple's Macs are not susceptible to this type of spyware at the time of publication.) Keep in mind that key loggers may cause a great deal of anxiety for teenagers who may think that parents who use this software are spying on them. It is far easier with younger children to install a key logger and then explain to your child "I am your mother/father and it is my job to keep you safe. This software helps me do just that." However, key loggers definitely should be used if a parent suspects that their child is engaging in seriously risky behavior.

Some products combine aspects of two or all three of the above types of software. In addition to the features described above, many quality products also provide additional safeguards such as:

1. Monitoring chat conversations for certain phrases or words.

2. Locking Internet access or the use of certain computer programs.

3. Preventing use of "peer-to-peer" (P2P) file sharing software such as Limewire or KaZaA.

4. Preventing access to certain types of streaming media across the Internet such as video.

Quality products also enable parents to set up accounts differently for each child who has a log-in account on a computer.

This makes sense as the rules a parent will likely set up for a 16-year-old, for example, will be different than those for a 12-year-old or 7-year-old. However, it does a parent no good if the 7-year-old knows how to get into the 16-year-old's computer account. Or if any of the children know how to bypass the filters by logging in as mom or dad! Also remember that <u>each</u> computer with Internet access in your house will need to have protective software installed. Some software companies will offer a discount for multiple purchases.

If you would like to see other descriptions and general reviews of parental control software, try these links:

http://products.howstuffworks.com/web-filtering-software-buying-guide.htm

http://top-parental-control-software.com/

http://www.internet-filter-review.toptenreviews.com/

Don't be scared away if you have no computer skills. You can call any quality company and tell them that you want to buy their software but don't have the skills to install it or set it up properly. Ask them to help you download the software, install it and then set it up for your children.

Finally, Apple's new operating system 10.5 and Windows Vista both include some type of parental controls. However, it is our opinion that the parental controls available are not as good as some of the products designed for this purpose. They can, however, provide another layer of protection. Apple's OS 10.5, for example, enables parents to set time limits on Internet access, block certain web sites and even lock down instant messaging.

Sampling of software products:

What follows is a sampling of products and is not meant to be an exhaustive list. This list is based upon our web research, conversations with parents who have used these products and reviews we've found in blogs and online forums. We have not personally tested the products below and, therefore, this is not a recommended list based on first-hand experience.

Web Filtering Software (includes many other features as well):

Mac

Content Barrier: www.intego.com/contentbarrier

Safe Eyes: www.safeeyes.com

PC

CyberPatrol: www.cyberpatrol.com

NetNanny: www.netnanny.com

Safe Eyes: www.safeeyes.com

Firefox

Firefox is a free web browser available for Macs and PCs and is often described as being more secure than Internet Explorer or Safari. It has many "Add-Ons" that can be installed for free. Some enable features such as the ability to filter web content and make web browsing more secure. Visit the add-ons available for "Browse Privacy and Security" by visiting

https://addons.mozilla.org/en-US/firefox/browse/type:1/cat:12

A few specific examples include content filters and site blockers:

FoxFilter (for all platforms):

https://addons.mozilla.org/en-US/firefox/addon/4351

ProCon Latte (for all platforms):

https://addons.mozilla.org/en-US/firefox/addon/1803

LeechBlock (for all platforms):

https://addons.mozilla.org/en-US/firefox/addon/4476

Keep in mind that savvy teens can simply download and install another browser to by-pass the filtering that may be used by Firefox. These filters are therefore best used with younger children. Parents may also wish to consider listing themselves as administrators on their children's computer and to disable the ability of the child to install software without access to the parent's password.

Time Limiting Software:

Mac

MacMinder: www.macupdate.com/info.php/id/8806/mac-minder

NOTE: MacMinder is no longer in business but its software is still available and was last updated in August 2007.

Read a review of MacMinder:

www.applematters.com/article/mac-minder-a-parents-access-control-tool

Tutorial on setting up time-limiting parental controls in Apple's OS X Leopard:

www.tech-recipes.com/rx/2659/Fos_x_leopard_parental_controls_
limit_computer_usage_times

PC

PC Home Software. www.pchomesoft.com. They produce:

Kids PC Time Administrator

Parental Control Tool

PC Time Limit: www.pctimelimit.com

PC Time Manager: www.virtualsoftwareltd.com/products/
PCTimeManager

Key Loggers:

Mac

Mac Keylogger: www.keylogger-mac.com/mac-keylogger-perfect-
keylogger-for-mac-os-x.html

Perfect Key Logger: www.parental-controls-software.net

Spector:
www.spectorsoft.com/products/Spector_Macintosh

PC

Perfect Key Logger: www.parental-controls-software.net

Various types of loggers from Spectorsoft: www.spectorsoft.
com

Combination hardware-software filters for a family network:

It is not uncommon today for a household to have two, three or more computers. Installing and configuring parental-control software on each computer can be time-consuming as well as expensive. Some of the software manufacturers listed previously may offer a price-break on multiple licenses. There is, however, another option.

Instead of putting parental-control software on each and every computer, it is possible to put a filter at the point where the Internet enters the household and before it is distributed to all the home's computers. A variety of companies produce routers (wireless and wired) that connect a family's Internet connection to the family network. These routers can also offer some content filtering and firewall features. A firewall is hardware and/or software device that helps protect computers from intruders, malware, viruses and attacks from outside the network. However, the content filtering ability of these products varies markedly from the software products listed previously. In general, most of the filtering features fall behind the software products.

There is one specific product worth noting, though, because the manufacturer specifically targets the home network content filter to provide a useful tool for parents. The product is the iBoss from Phantom Technologies. [http://residential.iphantom. com/] The iBoss is a router, connecting multiple family computers, and allows parents to block sites using more than 26 predefined categories such as adult content, violence and drugs. It also enables parents to control chat, online gaming and instant messaging.

Besides the iBoss, hardware products tend to change often and details about their filtering ability are not widely available unless you call the company and ask a customer sales representative. Below are several other companies that have made routers with content filters in the past. If the iBoss is not your choice and another router solution interests you, call the company and inquire. You may already have a router that has some content filtering abilities. Please note, configuring content filtering on many of these routers is not as easy as the iBoss or software products mentioned previously.

Linksys	www.linksys.com
Netgear	www.netgear.com
ZyXel	www.zyxel.com

Here are two reviews, an older one from PC Magazine and a 2008 review from Prime Newswire, on several such content-filtering routers:

www.pcmag.com/article2/0,2817,1650669,00.asp

www.primenewswire.com/newsroom/news.html?d=135765

Additional parental controls worth noting:

iTunes:

Are you aware that iTunes includes parental controls? For example, these controls prevent children from accessing/downloading music with explicit lyrics or television programs rated PG-14. To find out more, visit Apple's website for directions:

http://support.apple.com/kb/HT1904

Search engines:

Almost every search engine contains the ability to try to reduce adult content that may appear in search results. However, not all search engines automatically turn on this feature. To learn how to turn on the built-in content filters found on most search engines, visit our article on this topic:

www.childrenonline.org/articles/Safe_Search.html

Note: Savvy older children can easily turn off the filters you turn on. This feature is therefore most helpful only for younger children. Also, it only applies to search results in a web browser at the specific web site being used.

An important note about anonymous proxies:

Parents need to be aware of the existence of anonymous proxies. These are web sites that mask or hide the web sites a visitor actually visits. When someone visits an anonymous proxy they can enter any web address into the proxy field. The proxy visits the requested web site and returns the page to the visitor. However, if you check the web browser's history, it will only show a visit to the proxy site, not the site requested from the proxy.

Many technology staff at schools across the United States have complained about teens using anonymous proxies to bypass school filters to access pornography or social networks. There are hundreds of proxy sites and sites are added every week. There is even an organization that supports the creation of anonymous proxies, citing first amendment rights as its principal motivation. Some anonymous proxies have names related to their function such as Anonymouse.org. Others are given names specifically to mask their intended purpose.

Fortunately, any quality web filter attempts to block access to anonymous proxies. However, doing so is a bit like a cat-and-mouse game. Filters block them and new sites are created. It is therefore a game of catch-up and filters will always be slightly behind in the game.

Keep in mind:

Though there are several online resources to help you evaluate whether or not certain websites are risky or safe to visit, these services cannot possibly expect to keep up with the speed of change on billions of Internet web pages. For example, Sophos.com, a respected Internet security company, estimates that 1.3% of the links that are produced in a typical Google search are infected with malware that triggers a "drive-by download" causing a computer to become infected.

SiteAdvisor.com is produced by the respected folks at McAfee. SiteAdvisor.com purports to rates sites "for spyware, spam, viruses and phishing so you can click with confidence." However, as reported in the February 12, 2009 Windows Newsletter by Brian Livingston, site ratings may be a year out-of-date. A year on the Internet is like 7 years in real life!

Chapter 14

Parenting Challenges in the New Age of Technology

Trying to keep up with today's technology can be overwhelming. Parents and teachers are left scrambling as they race to better understand the technology children are using. Every year children and teens explore new online gadgets, gimmicks, games and websites. In 2008 and 2009, for example, large numbers of teens began using cell phones to send naked or partially nude pictures to one another (a phenomenon called "sexting") while others began experimenting with live broadcasting sites to act out their own reality television shows in live time from their bedrooms using a webcam. Adults can feel overwhelmed by the unexpected uses of new technologies by children and teens.

Take a deep breath. In truth, for children and teens, much of what they do is not about the technology they are using. It is about seeking attention, forming and sustaining relationships, taking risks and having fun. Parents and teachers have been dealing with those behaviors for centuries. Parents often call us feeling scared, frustrated and overwhelmed as they try to react to their child's use of technology. Parents don't need to panic in the face of new gadgets but need to realize that the technology is another forum for their kids to reach out to others, to form identities, and to push boundaries. We recommend looking beyond the new gadget, website or technological tool and take a look at the activity their child is engaging in while using technology. Take a look at the issue facing your child and make decisions about setting boundaries and rules based on their developmental level. Our job as parents is to set limits according to developmental levels throughout our children's lives. Gates, for example, stop toddlers from exploring a kitchen. We hold hands with the 5-year-old when crossing streets and we follow our 10-year-old to the park when she rides her bike for the first time. Try to view technology in the same way. If your 10-year-old is broadcasting herself live from her bedroom, ask yourself if she is ready to face the risks of making herself public online where anyone who watches may contact her. Our recommendation is that the 10-year-old is not ready to face the many risks that lurk beyond their screen and not old enough to understand them. If your 16-year-old is sending provocative pictures via his cell phone, ask yourself if he understands the impact on others, as well as the consequences of "sexting." Does your teen realize that he may be breaking child pornography laws? Does your teen know that others who receive the pictures are likely to continue forwarding them or that these pictures can be used to embarrass and humiliate him?

Being a parent today with so much new technology is challenging. It is very hard to stay vigilant, understand all the risks and warn our kids about potential dangers, especially when the landscape keeps shifting. Keep in mind however, that we have been loving, guiding and nurturing our kids since they were infants. We are the keepers of our family's values. It has been, and continues to be, our job to keep them safe and growing up at a developmentally healthy pace. When faced with new and unknown influences, such as built-in cell phone cameras or laptop webcams, tell your children that you need to better understand the risks and issues regarding those influences before they use them. Then consider how well prepared your child is for dealing with the issues or whether or not they are developmentally healthy for your child to use. Should your 7-year-old, for example, be allowed chat with others on Club Penguin? The answer to that question may be based on your assessment about whether your 7-year-old is able to discriminate between "friends" online and others who may treat her badly. Can your 7-year-old be thoughtful, make decisions before acting and be nice online while playing a game? Is your 7-year-old ready for the curt and hurtful language that is common in online communications? Probably not, but parents have to be the final judge on what their own child can handle. Saying "no" to a child may not be what they want to hear but it is our job as parents to set limits and keep them safe.

At a school we visited in 2009, a group of sixth grade parents grew upset and anxious upon learning that some of their children's classmates had begun using Facebook. And though some parents were outraged and worried, others felt that this was the way of the world and it was OK to let them explore it. Parents must obviously make their own decisions about what is best for their child. We ask parents to consider age 16 as our recommendation for children using Facebook. This is due to the fact that children and teens are targeted with marketing scams, exposed to risks of identity theft because they don't understand the value of personal information and are easily manipulated by people who don't have their best interests in mind. With information and understanding, parents must make their own informed decisions about setting boundaries and assessing risks. Different families have different rules. But fundamentally, all parents create rules to help their children grow up in healthy and developmentally appropriate ways. Online, without our intervention or involvement, there are no rules or boundaries. Children are free to explore to the limits of their tolerance or until they are met with unexpected and damaging circumstances. In our many years of research and working with kids and Internet safety, the one overwhelming constant in this sea of change is that whatever kids are doing online this year, they will be doing the same thing next year at a younger age. Our children are growing up in a world online with no boundaries or regard for their safety and at a faster pace than is healthy for them.

We have all been parenting our kids for years and have a history of imparting values, making difficult decisions and setting limits for them. While translating these skills to the ever-changing use of technology can be daunting, take a deep breath. Talk to your kids, ask questions, research the issues involved and be a presence in their online world. Just as you decided when the pacifier should be thrown out, make a decision about the use of technology and don't assume that just because they can use it, they should. When we raise our kids in homes where we listen, impart values, make clear and consistent rules and love them, our kids grow up with fewer risks in their lives. Take heart, a deep breath and make decisions. You have been doing that well for years.

Chapter Resources:

1. SafetyClicks.com is a commercial resource from the folks at AOL. There are many good articles with guidelines and recommendations related to the challenges of parenting in this new age of technology. These include:

> When should you start the online safety conversation? By Diana Pentecost
> www.safetyclicks.com/2008/12/26/when-should-you-start-the-online-safety-conversation/

> House Rules for Online Safety. By Diana Pentecost
> www.safetyclicks.com/2008/09/03/house-rules-for-online-safety/

2. Enough is Enough is a non-profit organization devoted to making the Internet safer for children and families. Their website, Enough.org, has an excellent list of "Rules 'n Tools" for parents on Internet safety accompanied by interesting statis-

tics. They also offer many age-based guidelines for children and teens.

Rules 'N Tools Guidelines for Internet Safety
www.enough.org/inside.php?tag=rulesntools

Age-based Guidelines for Internet use
www.enough.org/inside.php?id=PJP0ORIPM

3. NetSmartz.org is an Internet safety resource from the National Center for Missing & Exploited Children. They produce Internet Safety Pledges, among other valuable resources for children and parents.

www.netsmartz.org/resources/pledge.htm

Appendix A

Glossary of Terms

Adware	Software that causes banner ads and pop-up ads. It is often hidden in and downloaded with freeware and installed without a user's knowledge or permission.
Archive	Long-term storage of information such as web site content.
Avatar	An icon that represents a user in games or chat rooms. The icon may be a graphic or a photo.
Blog	A form of online diary or journal. Short for "web log." One who blogs is called a blogger. Blogs can be updated at any time and are usually arranged in chronological order.
Browser	A software program that connects to the Internet (usually the World Wide Web). For example, Internet Explorer, Firefox, Safari and Opera.
Chain Letter	Spam email that asks, or demands, the recipient to forward the email to others. Chain letters often contain warnings if the recipient doesn't pass the message on to others. Some chain letters, called "scare-mail" can be frightening to children.

Chat	A form of online communication that is in real time. Chats are back-and-forth conversations usually conducted in acronyms.
	Users can meet online in locations called chat rooms or use chat client software such as iChat, MSN Messenger or AOL Instant Messenger (AIM).
Cookie	A piece of computer code sent by a web site to a user's web browser that stores information about the user's visit to the web site. Cookies can retain preferences requested by the user when visiting a web page. They can also reveal a great deal about the behavior of visitors to web sites and are sometimes used to track user's activities. Cookies can be removed from a user's web browser and managed by a variety of software products.
Copyright	Legal protection against copying material online.
Cyber	Online sex. (As in "Do you want to cyber?")
Cyberspace	The whole range of information and resources available on the Internet.
Domain	The primary "address" or name of a web site. For example, the domain for Children Online is ChildrenOnline.org. There is a handful of three-letter suffixes that indicate the type of domain such as ".org" for organization, ".gov" for the US government and ".com" for commercial sites.

Download	Transferring of files to software from a server or computer located somewhere on the Internet to a user's computer.
Email	Message, usually in text form, sent from one computer to another.
Emoticon	Symbols or small images that are meant to express feelings or emotions such as smiley faces or punctuation meant to resemble a face. For example, ;-)
Firewall	Computer hardware and/or software that separates computers. Firewalls are mean to protect computers and every home computing environment should have one. from the Internet for security purposes.
Flaming	Writing angry or hurtful words to a person online.
Freeware	Software that is offered for free. Freeware often requires personal information before it can be installed and, equally often, contains hidden adware or spyware.
Hacker	Though originally used as a term of respect, today it generally means one who breaks into a computer system or network to do damage.
Home page	The first, or top, web page a visitor is meant to arrive at for a web site. Analogous to a web site's front door.
Internet	A network of millions of computers and servers connected worldwide.

IRC	Internet Relay Chat. A program that allows users from all over the world to congregate in virtual rooms and chat.
Link	A clickable connection to a web page, document or other media that is embedded as text or as an image on a web page.
MUD	Multi-User Domain. Domains for multiple users for gaming, social gatherings and entertainment. For example, Dungeons and Dragons
Page	A document displayed on the web. A page may consist of multiple screens accessed by scrolling the page.
Server	A computer in a network that provides resources to other computers in the network such as programs, web pages, data or other files and services.
Shareware	Software that is offered for free but requests payments for use. Some shareware contains limited features that are unlocked after payment is received.
Site	A host on the Internet that consists of one or more web pages under a common domain name.
Social engineering	The term for tricking users to inadvertently reveal passwords and other personal information that can be used to gain entry to the user's personal online accounts.

Spam	Unwanted solicitations or marketing messages received in email.
Spim	Unwanted solicitations or marketing messages received on cell phones or in instant messages.
Spyware	Malicious software secretly installed on a computer to capture information about users such as passwords and personal information useful for identity theft. (Also called Malware.) Spyware that specifically records every keystroke a user enters on the computer is called a Key Logger. Many spam messages we receive contain links or attachments that cause spyware to be installed on our computers when the link is clicked or the file is downloaded.
Surfing	Exploring or browsing the Internet.
Trojan Horse	A malicious program that is hidden inside other software. Trojan horses can be hidden in .pdf documents, images and even mp3 music files. Trojan horses can plant viruses or spyware or can cause serious computer damage by themselves.
Virtual Reality	A computer simulation of a real three dimensional world.
Virus	A destructive program that has the ability to damage computer software and/or hardware.

Index

This index is not meant to be a comprehensive collection of every occurrence of these words in this book. Instead, this is meant to be a reference to key concepts and guidelines.